D0804330

THE ESSENTIAL
SUPERVISOR'S
HANDBOOK

A Quick and Handy Guide for
Any Manager or Business Owner

✓ Build a Productive, Motivated Team
✓ Develop a Management Style That Works for You
✓ Get the Most From Your Employees

Brette McWhorter Sember
and Terrence J. Sember

CAREER
PRESS
Franklin Lakes, NJ

THE ESSENTIAL SUPERVISOR'S HANDBOOK
EDITED BY GINA TALUCCI
TYPESET BY EILEEN DOW MUNSON
Cover design by Jeff Piasky
Printed in the U.S.A. by Book-mart Press

To order this title, please call toll-free 1-800-CAREER-1 (NJ and
Canada: 201-848-0310) to order using VISA or MasterCard, or for
further information on books from Career Press.

CAREER
PRESS

The Career Press, Inc., 3 Tice Road, PO Box 687,
Franklin Lakes, NJ 07417
www.careerpress.com

Library of Congress Cataloging-in-Publication Data

Sember, Brette McWhorter, 1968-
    The Essential supervisor's handbook / by Brette McWhorter Sember
and Terrence J. Sember.
        p.cm.
    ISBN-13: 978-1-56414-893-3
    ISBN-10: 1-56414-893-9
        1. Supervision of employees—Handbooks, manuals, etc. I. Sember,
Terrence J. II. Title.

HF5549.17.S46 2007
658.3′02--dc22

                                                              2006022100

Contents

Introduction

Congratulations on your role as supervisor! Whether you've just been promoted, hired, or have been a supervisor for a while, this book is your complete guide to becoming successful in your job. Taking on a supervisor job is an exciting change and one that brings a lot of responsibility. Suddenly, you're in charge of not only your own job, but all the employees on your team as well. If you have never been a supervisor before, this can be quite a change, and may feel overwhelming.

A job as a manager is a people-intensive job. You are the person your employees will come to with decisions, problems, and questions. You are also the person your boss will look to for results and profitability. Meanwhile, you're in the middle, trying to satisfy everyone's needs, do your own job, and keep an eye on what's best for the company in general. It can be hard to juggle all of these things and be pulled in so many directions at once.

The Essential Supervisor's Handbook

Perhaps the most important thing you need to know is that becoming a successful manager means learning to manage yourself just as much as it means managing other people. Your team will not succeed if you have not first learned how to create a plan for yourself. Throughout the book, look for our Manage Yourself tips. The purpose of this book is to help you learn how to manage yourself, as well as your team, so that you can function as a cohesive whole.

Our goal is to provide you with the tools you need to succeed at each portion of your job, so that you, your team, and your company can reap the rewards. These skills include time management, flexibility, installing smart procedures, problem-solving, motivating employees, focusing your team, working with clients and vendors, and creating a workplace atmosphere that is conducive to success. Throughout the book you will find lists of essential steps to further your success.

The key to successful management is relationships. The relationships you create and maintain with your employees, coworkers, boss, and clients are what will define you as a supervisor. This book guides you through relationship building and maintenance throughout your career as a supervisor so that you can create a structure that supports you and benefits your company. The foundation of a relationship is communication, and this guide offers management communication essentials to help you say what you mean and get your message across.

Introduction

As a supervisor you will face a host of responsibilities. You may run meetings, oversee purchases, offer regular performance reviews to employees, oversee work, prepare reports, hire and fire employees, assign tasks, handle complaints, and adjust work procedures. These may be brand new responsibilities that you've never dealt with before, or they may be things you've dealt with in the past but wish to improve. This book will not only lay out exactly how to do all of these tasks, but help you do them with confidence and success.

There are many books about how to start your job as supervisor, but we go the extra mile and talk not only about how to come into the job and get started, but how to continue down the path to success once you've settled into the job, because your goal is not only to adjust to your new position, but to have continued success. We hope that as you learn to manage yourself and others, you find satisfaction and rewards at every step of the process.

Chapter 1

The Basics of Leading

Starting out as a supervisor, you are probably excited, but may feel slightly overwhelmed. Settling into a new job is always difficult, but taking on a job with new management responsibilities is an additional challenge. To learn to be a leader, you need to grasp on some basic management techniques. You don't have to have an MBA to be able to direct other people and manage their work; management techniques are things that anyone can learn. All you need is a little common sense and some insight into how to make things go smoothly.

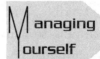

Managing Yourself

Evaluate Yourself

It is always important to assess the skills and abilities of those you manage, but the same applies to yourself.

The Essential Supervisor's Handbook

To be a successful supervisor, you must first evaluate your own skills and abilities. Create a list of all the duties and responsibilities your position includes. If you haven't started your new job yet and aren't sure what these are, you can come back to this section and complete it later. This can include coaching and counseling employees, writing reports, attending conferences, monitoring daily production, or reading and responding to e-mail. Use the chart on page 13 to list your basic responsibilities.

When you have listed all the things you'll be responsible for in your position, take a moment and rate your ability at each task. Give yourself a rating of "excellent," "good," "fair," "poor," or "terrible." For example, if one of your responsibilities is reconciling register drawers with accounting (and you know you are not very good with math), you might rate yourself with "poor." If you are required to hold meetings and feel you are a good public speaker, but find you have a little bit of trouble keeping meetings on task, you might give yourself a "good" for that type of responsibility.

Once you have rated yourself, go through all the tasks for which you rated yourself fair, poor, or terrible, and write down what possible avenues are available to you for improving your skills in that area. You might take additional training, talk to a mentor, practice skills outside the workplace, or follow other avenues to improve your abilities. Now assess how realistic it is that you

Task/Responsibility	Rating	Improvements
_____	_____	_____
_____	_____	_____
_____	_____	_____
_____	_____	_____
_____	_____	_____
_____	_____	_____
_____	_____	_____
_____	_____	_____
_____	_____	_____
_____	_____	_____
_____	_____	_____
_____	_____	_____
_____	_____	_____
_____	_____	_____
_____	_____	_____
_____	_____	_____
_____	_____	_____
_____	_____	_____
_____	_____	_____
_____	_____	_____
_____	_____	_____
_____	_____	_____

will be able to follow through on what would be necessary to improve those skills. Cross out the things that you most likely would never do. If it's unlikely you'll ever join Toastmasters to improve your public speaking, then cross out that option.

What you'll be left with is a very good outline of your management abilities and possibilities. The items you marked good or excellent are your strengths; you should capitalize on your strengths and use them to your advantage. They are probably the things that got you where you are today, and you want to continue to let these skills move you forward.

Skills that you have listed possible improvements for, which you did not cross out, are realistic things you can do to improve your capabilities. These are realistic steps you can take to further yourself as a manager. Make a plan for how you will improve these skills.

The skills you ranked as needing improvement, but felt it was unrealistic that you would take steps toward improving, are your weaknesses. We all have weaknesses—after all, you can't excel at everything. Part of being successful in business is recognizing your weaknesses and finding ways to overcome them. Overcoming weaknesses does not mean throwing up your hands in the air and saying, "Oh well, I'm terrible at responding to e-mails, so I'm just not going to use e-mail."

Essential elements for overcoming weaknesses:

☑ **Learn skills you are lacking.** As addressed previously, you can get help to improve yourself. One common mistake people make is thinking that it will take too much work or time to improve a skill. However, there are small things you can do to make a difference. You may not need to take a semester-long course to improve your computer skills; there might be a weekend course you could take that would teach you enough to offer significant improvement.

☑ **Delegate tasks to others who are skilled at them.** If there is an important operation of your department or team, but you are not the best person to handle it, delegate it to someone who is. Not only must you be able to recognize your own strengths, but you should be able to spot your employee's strengths as well, and use them to benefit your team. A highly effective team is one that maximizes the strengths of every team member.

☑ **Don't denigrate yourself.** Stop beating yourself up for your weaknesses. You aren't perfect and you never will be. Think positively and keep reminding yourself of your strengths.

☑ **Use strengths to counter weaknesses.** Oftentimes there are strengths that can be used to counterbalance or compensate for weaknesses. If you are terrible at writing cohesive memos, you might counterbalance this weakness by holding good meetings. Look for things you are good at that can take the place of things you are not good at. Arrange things so that your job revolves around your strengths whenever possible.

10 Essential Strengths for a Supervisor

✓ Flexibility

✓ Sincerity

✓ Honesty

✓ Empathy

✓ Organization

✓ Willingness to learn

✓ Confidence

✓ Focus

✓ Openness to new ideas

✓ Consistency

Evaluate Your Position

Whether you are entering a new company (or a new position within the same company), one of your first tasks as a supervisor must be to understand your new responsibilities. Here are some essential steps to acclimate yourself to a new job:

➡ Read all employee and manager's handbooks and policies.

➡ Read your job description and any descriptions of the role or tasks for which your team is responsible.

➡ Read any memos detailing restructuring that led to the creation of your department or job.

➡ Talk to your own supervisor and learn what his or her goals are for your team. Get inside his or her head to find out what exactly the company needs you to do.

➡ Clarify your role within the company hierarchy so that you are clear on what you have control over and to whom you report.

➡ Learn and understand standard operating procedures.

It can also be very helpful to talk to your human resources department to learn procedures for hiring, documenting employee mistakes, firing, and time off. Talking to other managers can offer insight into how things are handled within the company. Remember that it just takes time to learn your way around a new job and a new company. You can't expect to pick it up overnight; learning the ropes is a gradual process.

Managing Yourself

Get Into Management Mode

Before you can manage or lead anyone else, you must first learn to successfully manage yourself. Now that you are in a supervisor's position, you have achieved some success. To this point, you've managed yourself and your career quite well. But now that you must manage other people as well, it's time to take a step back and examine how you can manage yourself so that you become a good supervisor.

Essential supervisory steps:

☑ **Take control of your emotions.** You're still a person with feelings, but now you must be certain that your anger, frustration, tiredness, and so on do not overly impact those you are managing. When faced with a stressful situation, take a deep breath before speaking or reacting. Thinking before you speak will allow you to sift out inappropriate reactions. Apply this same rule to e-mail communication as well. It's very easy to shoot out a quick message or reply to something in the heat of the moment, when instead you should have given the problem more thought or censored yourself better. Build in a delay on the delivery time of emails that go into your outbox so that you have time to reconsider things.

☑ **Understand your goals.** You should have a grasp on what you want to attain at all times. Any time you are about to do something, ask yourself if this action will bring you closer to attaining your goal.

This can be particularly helpful when you are deciding whether or not to confront someone. If it does not bring you closer to your goal, you have no reason to do it.

☑ **Focus on work.** When you're at work, your job is to try and handle most things in a calm and pleasant manner (unless it is strategically useful to display annoyance in a business situation), no matter what is happening in your head or in your personal life. Managing your emotions also means managing your happy feelings, too. You don't want to let exuberance or excitement spill out at work in situations where it is not appropriate or helpful. The bottom line is that when you're at work, you should be reacting to what is happening at work. This means learning to compartmentalize your life.

☑ **Plan to be successful.** It's completely normal to feel a bit nervous coming into a new position, but you have to be in control of your nerves and exert a confidence you may not have yet. Your goal is to be a successful supervisor, so for the meantime, simply act as if you are one. No one needs to know your doubts; as you settle into your job, the nerves will dissipate. Some management experts restate this rule as, "Plan your work and work your plan." Create a plan for yourself that will allow you to become successful. Following your plan will give you a sense of control and order and will make it easier for you to achieve goals and bring success to your team and your company.

☑ **Dress the part.** Notice how other supervisors at your level dress, and begin to dress that way. Dressing similar to other managers may make you feel like one of the gang, but it does not send the subtle message to your own supervisors that you should be taken seriously (casual Fridays or days where you can wear jeans are different and perfectly acceptable as long as it is something management participates in as well. If you overdress for your position it may appear foolish to those below you and threatening to those above you.

☑ **Set the example.** One of the important tasks of a supervisor is to model behavior for employees. If you are often late, keep a messy office, ignore deadlines, or treat other people poorly, you are creating an environment where these kinds of behaviors are acceptable. Part of what you must do is present the behavior you would prefer to see from your employees. This may mean making changes in your own work habits, but it will be worthwhile. Part of setting an example is making sure that what you say and what you do are in synch. Your employees are not going to listen to you if you chide them for missing deadlines if *you* often miss deadlines. Match your words and your behavior to create a good example.

☑ **Develop relationships with those above you.** It's likely that you are hoping to be promoted in the future. Achieving success in your current position is an essential component of that, but so is building bridges within the company. You should get to know other supervisors and higher level managers and develop friendships. These are the people who will promote you. You may also want to focus on developing a special mentor relationship with a higher management person so that he or she can groom you for future promotions.

☑ **Develop relationships with peers.** In addition to developing relationships with your higher-ups, you also should develop relationships among supervisors or managers who are at the same level as you are in the company. Some of these may be competition for your next promotion, and it never hurts to know your competitor. Whether or not you are competitors, developing camaraderie with similarly-positioned supervisors in your company can offer friendships, as well as people to turn to with questions or concerns that you might not want to address with your own manager.

☑ **Stay current.** You need to stay on top of developments in your industry. To do so, join associations or subscribe to newsletters that will offer you information and developments. Business does not happen in a vacuum, and you need to be aware of what else is happening in your sector. Joining an industry specific management organization can also be a very helpful way to make contacts and share information.

☑ **Don't ignore problems.** It can be easy to push problems to the side and simply never deal with them, whether you are experiencing personnel, equipment, supply, financial, or other problems. Ignoring a problem won't make it go away, or even reduce it in size. Instead, it could grow bigger and create more difficulties for you. If a problem you are facing seems too big for you to face or deal with, get help with it. Turn to your supervisor, get team input, or talk to colleagues. You don't have to deal with it immediately, but you do have to actively work on solving it eventually.

Create a Positive Environment

Think about the different jobs you have had in your life. Which ones did you enjoy the most? It is likely that you were happiest in the positions that were in a positive work environment. The environment of an office or workplace is key to the attitudes of everyone who works there.

Imagine going on two different vacations. On the first one, you stay in a small, dark hotel room that has a peculiar smell. The view is terrible and the bed is uncomfortable. The front desk is unpleasant to you when you check in, and the bellman is rude. The maids snarl at you in the hallway, and the waiters ignore you.

Now compare this to the vacation where you stay in a comfortable, well-lit room with cheerful colors and thoughtful little touches, such as a coffee maker and a free shoeshine service. The front desk greets you by name and tells you to call if you have any questions. The bellman talks to you about the local attractions and shows you the amenities in the room. The maids turn down your bed each night and smile and say hello in the hallways. The waiters get to know you and are very attentive.

Which vacation would you want to be on? Clearly the second one, even if both are on the same beachfront location with the same terrific activities available. The physical environment in the second scenario, is pleasant and the people surrounding you are friendly. Everything about the place makes you feel positive. In the first scenario the physical environment drags you down, and the people you have contact with impart negativity at every turn. You can't help but feel depressed and unhappy, even though you are in the same locale with the same things available to you.

While we all know that a workplace is not a vacation (unfortunately), the same principles apply. A workplace that is physically comfortable and cheerful will positively impact the moods of the people who work there. And working with other happy people makes employees feel happy themselves. When striving to create a positive environment, remember that you're trying to set a general tone, and that every day will vary. You don't want to plaster a fake smile on your face every morning. Some days will be better than others for you and your team, and that's okay. Your goal is to create a setting that will most likely promote good feelings among your employees.

Essential steps to improving your physical environment:

☑ **Consider whether each employee has enough space.** Clearly, not everyone is going to have a spacious office. But people are happiest when they have an area of personal space. Arranging the office so that everyone has a little bit of elbow room can make things feel less pressured.

☑ **Manage relationships using space.** There may be certain employees who need to have easy access to each other because they work closely together. Placing their desks or work areas close to each other will facilitate the cooperation and interaction they need. Other times you may have employees who conflict with each other. Placing their areas farther apart can be conducive to reduced stress.

☑ **Pay attention to traffic flow.** If people coming to your department must move through a maze or squeeze through tight areas, things are probably not set up in the most convenient way. The traffic within the department must also flow, making it easy to get from Point A to Point B.

☑ **Maximize equipment.** You may not have a budget that allows the purchase of new furniture or equipment (and it's probably unlikely that you do). But there are ways to make the most of what you have:

➡ Don't leave a good chair sitting in a storeroom if one of your employees has a chair with a broken arm, for example.

➡ Place copiers and printers in areas that are accessible to all who use them.

➡ When possible, find out about getting office furniture repaired instead of replaced.

➡ Make sure you (or someone on your team) monitors the upkeep of equipment, and ensures that repairs happen quickly when necessary. Not getting the copier fixed sends the message that you don't care about the inconvenience it poses for your team.

☑ **Create respect for boundaries.** Allow each employee to have his or her personal space, and do not allow other employees to go through desks or files without permission. An exception to this is if employees have files, tools, or items that others need to access. In this situation, encourage employees to keep these items in an easily-accessible place on their desktop or workspace so that others can quickly access them. If your workplace is one large common area, such as a store or warehouse, make sure that there is respect for employees' lockers or personal storage spaces.

☑ **Encourage personality.** You don't need to be an interior decorator to bring some cheer to an office, and you don't need to do anything major. But you can infuse personality into the workplace with posters, plants, and product displays. This does not have to be limited to your own personal office space. Hang a few posters throughout the team area if it communicates your message. You should also encourage your workers to express their own personalities in their own individual work areas. Personalizing an area greatly increases its comfort and also increases employees' productivity. However, there must be a standard of professionalism that all employees adhere to when it comes to what type of items are appropriate in a workplace.

Defining Appropriate Workplace Décor

Encouraging employees to personalize their workspaces is important, but it can be difficult to get everyone on board with the right tone. Employees who fill their workspace to the point where they cannot work efficiently have gone too far. If an employee displays an item that others in the workplace might take offense to, then it is out of place. It is also important to go a step beyond this when considering items that could create an atmosphere of sexual harassment. If an employee displays a poster or screensaver that people might find offensive, it is out of place in the office. Politely asking the employee to remove the item in question with a brief explanation is the best solution. Don't make a big deal out of it or make it seem as if you are imposing a judgment on him or her. Instead simply state that the item doesn't fit with the image the company is trying to project.

☑ **Create a community.** A bulletin board can be one of the easiest and most successful ways to have an impact on your workplace. A bulletin board dedicated to employees' personal lives with photos, news, and personal tidbits can make people feel as though they are part of a community. The key to a successful bulletin board is constant updating. If you put one up and then let it gather dust, it becomes a sign of a lack of follow through with projects that are important to the team.

27

☑ **Manage common areas.** If there is a shared break room, a common workbench, or other area that all employees use, keep this area clean, neutral, and comfortable so that all employees can use it and enjoy it. Set the standard that people are expected to pick up after themselves in this area.

☑ **Use the environment to inspire.** There are several things you can do to your physical work area to motivate your employees. If you work in a factory or warehouse, signs applauding employees for so many accident free days can increase morale. Carefully placed artwork, signs, and posters can create the atmosphere you are looking for. You can also use competitors' products to motivate your team. Putting up a competitor's poster that lauds them as being "The #1 office chair producer" can have a good result on your own team's productivity, because it inspires competitveness.

☑ **Offer food.** Food is one of the most important tools you can use as a manager. Having a full stomach makes people feel satisfied and happier. Eating together promotes camaraderie and gives employees time to make connections with each other. Providing an occasional snack or paying for a lunch now and then can help your employees feel appreciated and make the office feel more welcoming. These do not need to be elaborate setups. If you have a small budget, you're not going to want to spring for lunch at a restaurant for your entire group. Bringing in some cookies once in while is enough; you can also encourage employees to bring in food themselves.

The key to using food effectively is for it not to become a planned event. If everyone knows you bring donuts to the Friday morning meeting, it becomes an expectation and not a surprise (and can also become a burden that you resent). To generate good will, the food must appear to be unexpected and spontaneous. It is also a good idea to praise employees who bring food in without being asked; this creates an atmosphere of sharing.

Improving the Human Environment

Now that you know how to improve your physical work environment, let's focus on how to improve the human environment.

Save criticism for private meetings. Many managers make the mistake of criticizing employees in front of others. This can cause resentment and embarrassment, as well as create an environment of fear. Instead, have your conversations in private. Praising employees is a good thing to do in public, however you must be careful— unless you distribute praise evenly, you may end up with disgruntled employees who feel they aren't being praised enough.

To be a successful manager you must become like-able. To do this, you must learn to be reasonable. You need to get to know your employees and develop connections with them so they learn to like you. You must be friendly and open with them, and share enough about your life so that the connection goes both ways. You need to be open to different personalities and objectives and learn how to bridge the gap between employees who do not get along.

The key to being liked by your employees is to be sincere. Interact on the personal level to the extent you feel comfortable. If it's not sincere and real, it will come off as fake; this will damage morale instead of improving it. You have to find your own comfort zone with your employees. If you're comfortable chatting about baseball and football games and feel uncomfortable when people talk about their kids or sick mothers, then try to stay in your comfort zone, while still reaching out to your employees so that they can respond in kind to your conversations.

Your office can't be all business all the time, and there is definitely a time and a place for informal conversations, gossip, and socializing. Allowing a few minutes of chitchat between coworkers at the beginning of a meeting or during the day is essential to keeping you connected to each other. Small talk must be managed though, because if you let it run rampant, it can get in the way of deadlines, goals, and objectives. Control small talk so that it serves the purpose of establishing common bonds, but does not spill over and impact productivity.

If you encounter some employees who are over-engaging in small talk, it might be tempting to go over and say, "Get back to work." A better alternative is to come over and interrupt with a work-related question. This is a signal that they need to refocus on the task at hand.

Although there is room for pleasantries and fun, there is no room for insults, sexual remarks of any kind (even if the workplace is all male or all female), harassment, or overt negativity. If you see it or hear it, and allow it to continue, you condone it. Set ground rules for your team and stick to them. It is important that you read your employee handbook so you understand exactly what the company's policy is on this kind of behavior. If there is no company-wide policy about sexual harassment, create one for your team.

Creating a team or group of employees that approach their work in a positive way is a manager's pathway to productivity. Boosting morale is not as simple as giving pep talks and providing incentives (although these are helpful). Morale is a general feeling of happiness in the workplace. Perhaps the biggest blow to morale is inconsistent management. Managers who make promises or create plans and then never follow through with them are unable to generate any excitement among their employees. Morale is also deteriorated by general feelings of unease about the future. Create a plan that creates certainty about where the team is heading. Another morale buster is a feeling of complete detachment between what happens and what the employees think. Encourage your team members to come to you with questions or comments. Listen to them and show them that their comments have meaning to you. When employees feel vested in the outcome, morale is improved.

Your role as supervisor is to see the big picture, but your employees are focused on their individual tasks and responsibilities. Take the time to make the big picture a reality for them. For example, show how a jump in departmental productivity has increased company profits, or point out the total number of customer service complaints that were adequately addressed by the team. When showing the big picture, you want to be careful not to concern your employees with things they can't impact. Team members should not be worrying about whether the HR department is choosing the most cost effective health plan, for example. You should encourage your employees to offer their comments and suggestions, but also remind them that people in other parts of the company are skilled at their jobs and often cannot explain every decision to other divisions. Everyone must learn to trust the other sectors of the company.

The Jerk Effect

You might be scratching your head and thinking that you've certainly known some managers who are not friendly and personable. How did they achieve success if this book insists being friendly is an important component of supervising? How you behave is your choice and your free will. If you want to implement a management style that uses fear, threats, and gruffness to achieve goals, that is your choice. Certainly, this is effective for some people, but we can't help wondering whether those people might not be more effective if they were a bit friendlier. Ultimately, the choice is yours, but our caveat is that it must be your choice. Make a conscious decision to do things in a way you are comfortable with and then live with the consequences. Five years from now if you're changing a tire in the rain on the side of a deserted road, do you want your employees to floor it when they see you, or stop and help? If you'd rather they kept on driving, then that is your prerogative. In our experience, you will certainly catch more flies with honey than with vinegar in almost every situation.

Set Objectives

In order to achieve success, there must be an identifiable goal that can be reached. Your role as a manager is to create these goals and point out the pathways to achieving them. Some objectives are easy to pinpoint—fulfilling orders or selling a certain amount within a specific period. Others are more nebulous and require skills.

Essential components of creating objectives:

☑ **Consider history.** A van conversion company that has had an objective of producing five vans per week, but has only met that objective once in the past two years is not working with a realistic goal. Look at what your team has been able to produce or accomplish in the past and set your benchmark by gently stretching that output. In this example, a goal of producing three vans per week might be more realistic.

☑ **Be realistic.** Of course you want your team to reach for the stars, and objectives should be something your team has to stretch for, but you do not want to set an objective that is impossible. Your workers will end up discouraged. If the status quo is 2 percent growth per year and you set a goal of 25 percent, it is unlikely that goal is going to be attainable, and it's likely your people will not even make a real effort to meet it.

☑ **Be clear.** If you just encourage your employees to do better or try harder, you aren't offering them any concrete and clear objectives. It's very difficult to get results with generalized objectives. Offer some definitive and specific ways to improve instead.

☑ **Set small goals.** If you are number four in the market, don't set your sights on becoming number one. Instead, focus on becoming number three. Small steps are easier to achieve and offer more opportunities for success. You can string many small steps together into large successes. Employees also respond better to smaller goals because they feel more attainable.

☑ **Make sure objectives are challenging, yet within reach.** As a leader, you must achieve a balance in what you ask your employees for. If you set goals that are too high, no one will reach for them. Likewise, if you set goals that are too low, there will be no challenge and no feeling of having met a challenge. You must set objectives that fall between the two extremes, so that employees face challenges they can meet.

☑ **Set a timeline.** Objectives have no meaning if they are laid out in a vacuum. Asking your team to cut costs by 3 percent sounds great, but unless you specify that you want this to occur within six months, it has no meaning and has no accountability. Create a timeline where milestone events occur should and follow that timeline carefully.

☑ **See the big picture.** Understand how the other parts of the business are working so that your team can be as effective as possible. Don't be so myopic that you don't take into account what is happening in other parts of the company.

Your role as a supervisor is not only to set team objectives, but also to create individual objectives for each employee. This is discussed further in Chapter 2.

Why Goals Are Important

If you and your team are standing still, you are actually moving backwards. The company or team that is not constantly seeking to move forward and excel will lose ground simply because their competitors are moving ahead. Your objective cannot be to maintain the status quo. You must always be thinking about how you can improve your team and your results.

Delegation

A supervisor is a team leader. If you lead a team, you can't do every task the team is responsible for because one person simply doesn't have enough hands or enough time. A supervisor's role is to step back and make sure that every job within the department gets done by the appropriate person and that the team as a whole functions well; this may mean deciding who is best suited to each task. It may also mean shifting responsibility for certain tasks if they aren't being adequately performed.

Some people believe that a manager must know how to do every job that is done within the department. In today's specialized careers though, that is unrealistic. However, a manager should be able to understand every single task and the skills required to accomplish it. He or she should also have an understanding of the degree of difficulty for each task, as well as an appreciation for the knowledge it requires. A team leader must understand how that job or task impacts the rest of the team and the overall objectives.

It can be very tempting to throw yourself into the mix as another pair of hands. In rare times of crisis, this is a good strategy, however you can't focus on your own job duties if you're spending every Friday afternoon helping with shipping. Instead you must place yourself in the position of managing and directing activity.

The level of delegation that you use can change, and should change, depending on the type of task, the timeline, and the skill involved; there are some critical tasks that should be done by the leader. You need to evaluate each task to determine the appropriate level of delegation. Prioritize how critical that component is and give it your time and resources as applicable.

Essential steps to effective delegation:

☑ **Learn your employees' strengths.** You want to assign a task to a person who knows how to accomplish it and not to a person who will struggle. That being said, it is appropriate to ask an employee to stretch a little to accomplish a task. Your job is to assign it to an employee who is able to successfully stretch for that particular task. You want the right person for the right task at the right time.

☑ **Don't over-manage.** When you assign a task, you must assign it and let it go. It's fine to check in occasionally, particularly if it is an important or lengthy task, but your goal should be to hand off a task and not have to deal with it until it is complete, until it reaches certain milestones, or there is a problem that requires your intervention. This requires you to have faith and confidence in your employees and the discipline to turn it over and walk away.

☑ **Follow through on your end.** If you say that you need to see the first phase of the project by Tuesday, make sure you ask for it on Tuesday and review it then. You must demonstrate your commitment and credibility to the task and the deadline in order to expect the same from the person you have delegated to. If you personally need to contribute certain elements to the task, do so in a timely manner. You can't expect an employee to fulfill requirements if you can't. By not taking a task seriously enough to hold up your end, you denigrate the work the employee is doing on it.

☑ **Do set expectations.** When you delegate something, you need to offer a clear explanation of what needs to be done, create a deadline, and then ask your employee if he or she has any questions. Take the time to talk through the work completely. Doing so will save you time and frustration later.

☑ **Don't be afraid to delegate.** Sometimes it is easy to think that you can get things done faster and better than your employees. Even if you know that you could do a job more efficiently than someone else, keeping that job for yourself is just going to infringe on your own duties and responsibilities. Sometimes being a manager means you must pass off something that you can do better in the interest of freeing up your time to do management work. Focus on helping your employees learn how to do the work as well as you can.

☑ **It's not your way or the highway.** Sometimes supervisors delegate a task and expect it to be performed exactly as they would have done it. Be open to the fact that different people may have different methods or solutions that may end up being just as (or more) successful than your own method.

Essential Tips for Overseeing Others' Work:

☑ **Be matter of fact.** People can be defensive when they are being evaluated or watched. Act as if you are doing nothing out of the ordinary and have no particular feeling about the situation.

☑ **Be confident.** Your job is to oversee your employees. Checking up on them is part of what is required of you, so don't feel or act as though you are unsure about your right to do so.

☑ **Be consistent.** Regular checking in with one employee and never checking in with another is going to appear unfair. Try to apply the same general level of supervision to all employees as best you can.

☑ **Hands off.** It can be tempting to charge into the fold and take over when something isn't going the way you want. Your responsibility is not to do it yourself, but to help your employees do it the right way. This takes restraint and patience.

M anaging
Y ourself

Credibility

People give their best efforts when they work for someone they trust. A naval commander must receive the trust of all of his or her sailors in order for the ship's operations to run smoothly. Your work place may not be a ship, but the same principles apply. As a leader, you need to develop credibility. If you're coming into a new company (or even if you've moved up through the ranks), establishing credibility can be a tough nut to crack.

Credibility is not the same as likeability, nor is it the same thing as authority. Credibility is based upon respect. Getting to know your employees and establishing relationships with them creates likeability and earns respect. Setting boundaries and standing behind them in a fair way creates authority. Demonstrating that you make good decisions and have knowledge will earn you credibility.

E ssential components of credibility:

☑ **Show yourself to be reliable.** Inconsistency is dangerous. When you create a program or a plan, follow through and make sure others do, too. You should

41

apply policies in a consistent and predictable way. If you create a project management protocol, you must institute it and keep it running. A sign of a poor manager is too much implementation and not enough follow through.

☑ **Prove yourself to be honest and fair.** Don't play favorites among employees, and avoid making false statements. Don't assure your employees there will be no layoffs if you know there will be. Don't hand off the most important projects to the employee who has been one of your oldest friends.

☑ **Always answer questions.** Another aspect of being honest and fair is the way in which you handle your employees' questions. If you cannot directly answer a question, say so and don't be a politician. There will be circumstances where you will be unable to share the knowledge you have. For example, an employee may ask if there are going to be layoffs; you know there will be, but have been directed not to share that information. Or an employee may ask if your team landed a big client, and for legal and financial reasons you aren't able to share that information yet. Simply say that's a question you can't answer and move on.

☑ **Make decisions in a reasoned and thoughtful way that is not arbitrary.** This means that you examine a problem from all angles and consider all possibilities before making a call on it. Take the necessary time to make each decision. Some decisions must be made quickly, although often you have a minute or two to think about them.

☑ **Stick to your decisions.** Though it can be tempting to second guess yourself or change course midstream, most of the time it's best to try and follow through on a plan, unless some clear evidence to the contrary comes to light. Should this occur, you need to communicate the reason for the change to the people involved so that your reasoning is clear.

☑ **Consult other people and take their opinions into account when making a decision.** Part of leading a team is hearing the team. When confronting a decision, it makes sense to get input from the people who will be working on the project or situation. They may offer different perspectives. You need not agree with them or adopt their suggestions, but simply taking them into consideration will lead your employees to see you are levelheaded and trustworthy. Obviously, of course, there are times when all managers must make split-second decisions without input.

☑ **Be consistent in everything you do.** A supervisor who says that the company's main focus must be on sales numbers alone one day and customer service the next does not project a clear and consistent plan or vision. Likewise, a supervisor who suspends one employee for five late punch-ins and gives another employee with the same record another chance is not applying the same rules to every situation. The appearance of fairness is an important asset to a manager.

☑ **Make decisions that generally have good outcomes.** You can be consistent, fair, honest, and careful, but if you develop a track record of poor outcomes, it will be difficult for your employees to see you as a wise leader. Everyone makes bad calls once in a while, but it's particularly important when you enter a new position that you achieve some sure successes in the beginning to establish your record. If you can demonstrate a good track record over time, people will trust your judgment even if they disagree with it.

What Would They Do?

One technique that will help you become a better manager is to consider managers or supervisors you have had in the past, or whom you have known. Think about what they did well and what they did wrong. Try to learn from their mistakes, so that you don't have to replicate them. You may have had one manager in the past who you truly admired; use him or her as your guide in situations when you are unsure of what to do. Ask yourself, what would this manager have done in this situation? This can provide valuable guidance and direction to you in difficult times.

Vision

Having a vision for what you want your department or team to be (and to achieve) allows you to develop a clear path to success. Doing so allows you to set attainable goals and create progress paths to get to them.

Many supervisors have unclear visions. They know they want to succeed, make money, get promoted, or do a good job, but they don't have any specific goals that will lead them to those outcomes. A vision should be an overall direction or goal, but it is useless to you unless you're able to break it down into steps for yourself and your employees.

An overriding vision can help set a tone for your employees. If your ultimate goal is to double the staff in your warehouse, improve patient outcomes by 10 percent on your nursing ward, or achieve award-winning creative output, you can communicate this goal to your team, so that everyone is working toward the same outcome. A cohesive approach will allow your team to function cooperatively to achieve that goal.

A vision is worthless if it is unachievable, and can be harmful to employee morale if a manager sets up a vision that can never come true. There's nothing worse than giving your all for something that has no realistic chance of actually happening.

Essential components of choosing a vision for your team:

☑ **Think about what the company or team needs the most.** Take on a vision that meshes with upper management's ultimate goals. Be certain to consider the goals that were outlined for you when you were hired for the position.

☑ **Notice what can be improved.** Look for procedures, changes, and new directions. Notice the small things and then see if there is an underlying theme that ties it all together. If so, voilà, you have your vision!

☑ **Rely on industry benchmarks.** If you are unsure of what vision to pursue, look at progress as it is measured in your industry, such as Arbitron ratings in the radio industry. Seeking to improve an overall ranking such as this by a set amount can be an excellent vision.

☑ **Make it concrete.** Because a vision is just a larger form of an objective, it also needs to be concrete and grounded in a timeline. Saying that your vision is for the company to become great is too general.

☑ **Look for a little glory.** What will get you noticed and get your team the attention it deserves? It is okay to work toward a goal that will be praiseworthy. Everyone enjoys a job well done.

☑ **Think about what kind of goal your team is best equipped to achieve as it stands right now.** It is okay to develop other goals, but creating one that can be achieved easily can be the first in a string of successes. Look at the resources (such as people and materials) that you have to manage, and create a goal that utilizes those resources effectively.

☑ **Consider what kind of outcome you are most comfortable leading towards.** If you don't fully believe in the vision you set forth, you won't achieve it. Your goal must be one you can be excited about. Be energized and excited about the goal, and your team will feed off of that.

☑ **Wait for the right time to implement.** The first day you step into your new role as supervisor, you may already know what you want to achieve there. But when you first come into a job, you need to take some time to learn the ropes, get to know the people, and evaluate current systems. If you come in with guns blazing, you're likely to turn a lot of people off, and often be wrong about what needs to be done and how it should be handled.

There are many ways to break a vision into attainable steps. Take some time to consider your ultimate goal. Consider it from all angles and identify any obstacles. A vision is a well-thought out overall plan, not a quick take on something. Next, write a description. In order to explain something to employees, you must have the words to do so. Write down a two or three sentence description of your vision or plan so that you can easily discuss it with others.

Sit down and write out the steps that are needed to get your team to this goal. You may find that you need to create several projects, redirect focus, reorganize your workforce, and so on to get where you want to go. Taking the time to think all of this through before you start talking to employees will make you appear more organized and directed.

Most likely you will need to do things in phases to get to your ultimate goal. Create an implementation schedule and plan out what you want to have happen in each phase, and how long you anticipate each phase to take. Create benchmarks that will lead you to your ultimate goal. Because a vision is an overall goal, it may take a year or more to achieve it.

Achieve Profits

Unless you work for a non-profit organization (where your goal is likely providing as much service as possible) or in government (where your goal is likely efficiency or policy objectives), the reason your company or employer exists is to make a profit. Making money is the absolute bottom line, and, as a supervisor, it is your responsibility to ensure some level of profitability in your sector.

Making a profit is something that is important, but it can't be your only consideration. As a manager you also have to be responsible for the human factor—your employees. Achieving a balance between profit-seeking and human needs is a difficult proposition. If you lean too much in either direction, you'll be in trouble. Consider these two examples:

Manager Anna prided herself on being good to her employees. She often turned a blind eye to employees coming in late or leaving early, even though it seemed to be the same few people over and over again. Long lunches were common and she was always willing to let people take time off for a doctor appointment or family crisis, without affecting their personal or vacation time. It became clear to the employees that she rarely took a hard line about these things. Many appreciated having some slack, but a select few sought to take advantage of this attitude. Employee Dan often "worked at home" or came in late and left early. Manager Anna did nothing, even when people began to complain. Because not everyone was pulling their weight, even the good employees began to slack off as well. Why should they work hard when others weren't? Soon productivity was down. The team missed deadlines, lost some projects, and failed to get work done in the hours projected. Manager Anna was so laid back that she didn't worry about this, and instead congratulated herself for being such an understanding boss.

Manager Brian believed he was hired to bring that sector of the company into the black. He was very strict about the length of lunches and breaks. He was uninterested in getting to know his employees and instead spent all his time focusing on the numbers. He wanted to see employees work hard and produce more. He expected them to be accountable for every moment. Employee Cara got a call that her sister was in the hospital, so she went to the manager to ask if she could leave. The manager had no time to offer a condolence and instead wanted to know where certain projects were at and how this would affect the deadline. Employee Cara was docked for the time she missed work, down to the minute. Everyone in the office soon felt that Manager Brian only cared about numbers, not about people, and no one felt any motivation to work hard or go above and beyond for him.

These two managers are the extremes, but they certainly exemplify some of the approaches you will find in the workplace. Both scenarios wind up in the same place—with dissatisfied workers and decreased profit. You cannot achieve profit without supporting your employees. You also cannot keep your employees happy if you have no concern about profit.

Essential tips to increase profitability:

☑ **Keep it simple.** Minimize the use of resources and time whenever possible. Don't have a one hour meeting when 15 minutes will suffice. Don't let your employees wrap tape around boxes four times when once will suffice. Stick to what fills the need without exceeding it.

☑ **Get value for your work.** Make sure that your sales department understands the true cost of the work your team does. Share information about time and supplies so that everyone understands the true cost of work, so that it can be priced appropriately.

☑ **Look for ways to add profit.** Seek out small ways your team can increase profit. One way is to identify additional services you can provide. If you currently provide fulfillment services by packing and shipping boxes, adding a service in which you also add a customer's catalog or flyer is a small new service that can bring additional profit.

51

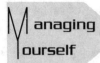

Managing Yourself

Finding Time for Your Work

As a supervisor you're going to spend a large portion of your time working with employees and their projects. However, you most certainly will have some work that is yours alone and which only you will be responsible for. When you spend most of your day focusing on other people, it can be difficult to find the time and energy to concentrate on your own work. Here are some suggestions:

- Set a time each day when you will concentrate on your own work. Build it into your schedule and try to stick to it as much as possible.

- Close the door to your office to get some physical and mental space from the rest of the workplace when you are going to work on your own items. If need be, adopt a policy that you should not be disturbed if your door is closed unless it is something important.

- Separate your work into segments if it is too much to do in one sitting. Do pieces at different times.

➡ Make a list of things you need to get done and cross items off as you accomplish them. This is useful not only for getting your own work done, but for overall management of the workplace.

Manage Time Effectively

Time management sounds like a very complicated management skill. In actuality, it just means working smart. If you get everything done that you need to get done, you are managing time effectively, but there is always room for improvement. As a manager, you need to manage your time as well as that of your employees. This is where things can get complicated. You're able to easily control how you personally spend your time, but it is more difficult to control how your employees manage their time.

Essential time management tips:

☑ **Keep it simple.** Don't use 12 words when two will do. Don't assign two people to a task when one can handle it. As with achieving profit, using the minimum will net you more time.

☑ **Set priority levels.** Make it clear when a project is urgent or important so that it is done within the necessary time frame. Also make sure your team understands which projects are not time sensitive so that they can push those aside to meet more pressing needs.

☑ **Do quick things.** If something comes up that you can accomplish quickly, do it right then and there. If the phone rings and you are free to answer it, do so instead of letting it go to voice mail. Getting small things out of the way helps clear the decks for the big important things.

☑ **Understand the work flow pipeline.** Have a good understanding of how work flows through your team or company so that you can predict what will happen in the future and be prepared for it.

☑ **Know your schedule.** If you know a plant inspection takes one hour, don't schedule something 45 minutes after it starts. You'll end up perpetually behind if you schedule things unrealistically.

☑ **Notice recurrences.** If you're always typing up a label with the same information on it, have them mass produced. Isolate things that are done over and over and try to consolidate them so they take less time.

☑ **Focus on goals.** As mentioned earlier in this chapter, if doing something will not bring you any closer to your goal, don't do it. It is a waste of time.

Understand Costs

For supervisors, understanding and controlling costs goes hand-in-hand with making profit. In most divisions there is no distinction, because reducing cost usually increases profit, but these are two different concepts that often require different management skills. There are many different things you can do to manage costs.

First, understand the different types of costs. Most people tend to think of concrete costs, such as the cost of supplies or materials that are used. In addition to this there is human cost—both emotional and time-related. As a manager you need to be sensitive about how much time your workers are spending on tasks, and look for ways to decrease that time. You also must be attuned to the emotional cost—the toll that work and policies place on your employees in a human sense. A team that is completely stressed out and overworked is going to make mistakes and produce unsatisfactory work, both of which will negatively impact your bottom line.

You will also need to measure the costs. Implementing a system (or using an existing one) that measures all concrete costs can help keep you focused on the right activities and identify where improvements can be made. Tracking software can help you identify and isolate costs and determine potential savings.

Part of your role is to understand what is purchased by whom and how to control those expenses. Become familiar with your department's vendors so that you can evaluate them and make informed decisions towards financial goals.

Be aware of costs to the company—even if you do not have direct accountability or budget control. What your team does impacts the company's bottom line. Therefore, it is part of your responsibility to educate yourself about these indirect costs, or costs you are not personally accountable for. For example, machine maintenance may not be part of your teams' costs, but it is a cost to the company. If a forklift is regularly abused by your team, this is creating cost to the company in terms of maintenance. It is also important to find out what exactly your supervisors expect from you in terms of these costs.

Work With Your Supervisor

When we think of management, we normally think of managing the people below us on the corporate ladder. The same rules that apply looking down the ladder also apply looking up. You must report to your supervisor, but you also want to display success, confidence, and comfort. Being a good employee requires some management techniques, such as:

- **Be clear and consistent.** When dealing with your own manager, present a consistent and reliable profile. Stress the same goals, share outcomes, and communicate clearly.

- **Take responsibility for your team.** As the leader, you need to step up and accept responsibility for your team's shortfalls. It is fine to discuss where the problem lies and how you are going to solve it, but you can't duck responsibility.

- **Get clear direction.** Obtain detailed expectations from your own manager. You can't meet his or her expectations if you don't know what they are, so take some time to find out where they see things going and what they are hoping you will achieve.

- **Be honest.** This should go without being said, but sometimes it is tempting to hide certain facts or concerns for fear that it will impact your own job performance. It is likely that it will all come to light eventually, so there is no reason to hide the facts. Then you'll not only have to explain the problem, but also explain why you hid it.

- **Ask for advice.** As a manager yourself, you know that it is satisfying when an employee comes to you to tap into your experience and knowledge. It's not only flattering, but it creates a bond between you. Go to your manager for input on important things. The input is bound to be very valuable to you, but the act of asking cements your relationship.

➡ **Express your ambitions.** Be sure to let your own boss know that you want to move up in the company. Sometimes it is to your advantage to let your boss know you want his or her job, but you need to gauge how your manager might respond to such an aggressive statement—this may be met with hostility. In either event, make it clear you have ambitions and want to succeed in the company.

Play a Supporting Role

Your job is to achieve success and meet your supervisor's objectives. Really though, this translates to helping your boss succeed. If you help your boss succeed, you will be rewarded for your efforts. Sometimes it is difficult to play a backstage role like this. You may feel like your boss takes the credit for all your great ideas and execution. It is more important to be a team player than to try to upstage your own supervisor. Doing so may gain you some recognition, but it will alienate your boss, who is your direct path to success. It will also alert management that you don't work well with others.

Chapter 2

Leading Employees

As a manger, a large part of your job is to manage each employee individually, in addition to managing the full team. Managing from the inside out can be a little trickier because you must work with each individual's differences and find ways to motivate different people in different jobs.

Get to Know Your Employees

Before you can manage someone, you have to understand them. When you take on a new position as a supervisor, you should familiarize yourself with each position within your team, such as:

- The skills needed.

- The hours required.

- How work and responsibilities change.

- The pitfalls or problems with the job.

If there are open positions, find out what the job responsibilities are, how they are being handled while the position is open, and when and how it will be filled.

You also will need to get to know each employee on a personal level if you are new to the department. If these are people you have not worked with before, you can't jump in and start issuing orders. To some extent you do need to take control of the situation the day you start, but before you make big changes or even begin to form an opinion about where you want things to go, try to get to know each employee. The first step is to read each employee's personnel file. You want to make note of:

- Their formal job description.

- Any formal disciplinary actions.

- The comments or notes from your predecessor.

- Any previous jobs the employee has held.

- The employee evaluations and reviews.

Once you've accomplished that, it may be helpful to set aside some time to talk to each employee individually, whether you schedule short chats in your office, or take each person out for a cup of coffee. Taking the employee out of the office lets you talk in a more comfortable setting and it is more likely that he or she will talk freely and offer better insights. Frame the meeting as a "getting to know each other" chat and have some general small talk to begin with. Then move into talking about the person's job and his or her feedback on that position, as well as the team or department as a whole.

If you have been promoted to a supervisor's position from within the company or department, you already know all the members of your team. Despite this, it is important to meet with each person separately in your new role. Your goal for the conversation is to listen as a manager and understand things about the employee and his or her position that might not have been clear to you earlier. If you already know these people, your goal should be to assess them with fresh eyes. You've only known them in one capacity—as coworkers—and while that may give you some insight, there are likely to be facets to the team members that you have not been aware of.

You will also want to address the employees' concerns about how your preexisting relationships within the company will affect your job from this point forward. If you have friendships within the department, employees may be worried about favoritism. Your role is to assure them that you are seeing everyone on an equal playing field. You'll want to let your employees who are also your friends understand that your primary concern at work must be the benefit of the company.

Once you have done all of the previously mentioned suggestions, you can begin to see how each employee fits into the team framework. You can probably already pinpoint the people who may be difficult and those who you will work well with. Keep an open mind however, because although you may not appreciate a certain employee's personality, they may have talent that is useful and important to your team. Putting all these pieces together will help you understand your team's dynamics and help you manage them more easily.

Friend or Boss?

Becoming a supervisor over someone who is your friend can be a confusing and delicate situation. Your friendship is important to you, yet at the same time, your job as supervisor is too. You need to find a way to balance the two. While at work, it is perfectly acceptable to still be friendly with friends. You can't suddenly act as if you don't know each other. But you can try to limit the inside jokes and the one-on-one time.

It is perfectly fine to socialize with friends who are also employees outside of work, but you want to be careful that you don't discuss things about work with your friend that he or she should not know. Also, you can no longer be in a situation where you can easily complain to each other about the people you work with.

Clearly enunciating your plan to your friend is the best way to work—otherwise he or she might feel slighted if the way you treat him or her changes at work. You also will need to be conscious to avoid favoritism. You may be able to rely on Maria to get the job done because she's your friend and you trust her, but she can't be your go-to person for everything, particularly things that are out of her area of responsibility. You also want to be careful to avoid the appearance of consulting your friend about other employees or work projects. All decisions and actions must be clearly your own in the eyes of your employees.

Set Individual Goals

Once you have settled into your position, and after you have set up some overall goals for your team, you will want to work with each employee individually to create personal goals. You may wish to set goals for everyone, or you may find it is more helpful to set goals in accordance with new projects or situations as they develop. When setting your individual goals, there are essential steps you can follow.

The first is to get input. Talk to your employee about the task at hand and ask what he or she feels is a reasonable expectation. Take this into consideration when creating your objectives.

Next, weigh the factors. Consider the responsibilities the employee is currently handling. If your graphic artist already has a large, important project underway, it may not be reasonable to expect him or her to complete another project at this time. Also look at what that employee's schedule is going to be in upcoming weeks. There may be a lull now, but a huge project scheduled for next week.

Also, whether you are setting an ultimate deadline, or creating separate milestones within a project, it is important that you offer a set timetable so that your employee understands what you expect and when. A timeline leaves no question as to when things must be completed, and allows your employee to plan his or her work.

Match tasks to people. If you have a choice as to the person you will assign a task to, look for someone who is suited for that particular assignment. This may mean a person has a particular aptitude for this type of work, or that the person has experience in this area. It may simply mean you choose someone who has enough enthusiasm to take on something new and unfamiliar.

Offer team members small new responsibilities. This will give you both an opportunity to see how good a fit it is. Once you've seen the team member in action and achieving success, you can feel more comfortable setting higher goals.

In addition to specific timelines and tasks, it can also be helpful to set behavioral goals that can impact an employee's job performance. For example, a salesperson who is not meeting her quota does not need you to point out that she's not meeting her quota. She needs a supervisor who can offer small steps that she can take to lead her to that larger goal, such as making more phone calls, doing more pre-sale research, and making sure she meets with decision-makers when asking people to buy.

In order to be able to help your employees stretch their boundaries and exceed, you need to learn their strengths and weaknesses. It may be helpful to ask your employees to complete the chart from Chapter 1 that evaluates strengths and weaknesses. You and your employee can go over what he or she can do to improve together. Look at the chart with a discerning eye and make sure that the things the employee has listed as strengths truly are (do so by observing job performance). Once you know an employee's strengths, you are better able to assign work that matches those strengths to him or her. When you do so, you will most likely increase productivity, and, hopefully, profit.

Providing Feedback

Offering feedback to employees is a cornerstone of management. Employees need to be praised for their achievements, and they need guidance to avoid repeating mistakes in the future. As a supervisor, you don't want to be too praise heavy or too criticism-oriented. Too much praise is essentially meaningless, thus reducing your management tools. Too much criticism damages morale and reduces effort. Striking the right balance may seem difficult, so in the beginning be cautious with both.

Essentials of effectively using praise:

☑ **Always be sincere.** Never put yourself in a position where you are complimenting an employee on something you don't feel deserves your attention or time. An insincere compliment is worse than no compliment. Instead, only provide positive feedback when you feel it has been earned and is warranted.

☑ **Do so in public.** A meeting may be a good time to single out people who have done good work. Praising employees in front of their peers is effective because the praise gives them a status boost. It is also effective because it motivates other employees to work harder so they too can and earn praise as well. Praising in public demonstrates to your employees that you want to reward good work and that you are an employer who seeks out excellence.

☑ **Be specific.** Simply saying "good job" might be nice, but specifically spelling out what he or she did well is important feedback. You should target the behavior, skill, or performance that was successful. This then becomes a learning tool for the employee you are rewarding, as well as your other team members. They will see this employee achieving success and being rewarded and will then be able to model this behavior. By highlighting one employee's success, you encourage everyone to reach their potential and you help them discern what kind of effort you are looking for.

☑ **Be sparing with rewards.** If you offered a raise to every employee who brought in a new client or completed a job under budget, your company would soon be in the red. Monetary rewards can be very effective, but they should be used only in the most unusual of circumstances, and usually only when you are rewarding years of achievement. Raises or bonuses are usually something you can only offer when you've been authorized by your company to do so.

☑ **Create inexpensive rewards.** There are other rewards that can be very effective, yet less expensive. Telling an employee to go home an hour or two early after leading a very successful training session can be rewarding. Creating an employee of the month spot on the office bulletin board or an employee of the month parking spot are also useful. You can also reward people by giving them new responsibilities or more important jobs. This displays your confidence in them and gives them the opportunity for further growth. Remember that a reward is anything that evokes a positive response in your employee and is linked in a cause and effect way to a job well done.

☑ **Don't confuse praise with simple courtesy.** When an employee takes the initiative and brings you a package from the mailroom, you should smile and thank him or her, but clearly this is not an event that requires recognition and an award. Use simple courtesy to thank employees for everyday work and don't overstep the bounds of the situation. Making use of these small interpersonal moments will earn you respect and credibility, but won't overload the praise.

Essential keys to using individual criticism effectively:

☑ **Do so in private.** Critiquing an employee in front of other team members paints you as a bad guy and embarrasses the employee. It is okay to say simple things, such as "Could you change this to a different color?" or "Oh, you forgot to include the spreadsheet, can you get it to me?" because they are small workday adjustments. Criticism that highlights an employee's shortcomings should be handled in private. Note that privacy not only means meeting out of the hearing of others, but also arranging the meeting in a way that does not broadcast to everyone what is about to happen. If the inventory Rob supervised comes back way off kilter, sticking your head out of your office and yelling, "Hey, Rob, get in here!" right after the report has been handed to you is a clear sign to everyone that Rob is about to get disciplined.

☑ **Rely on respect.** Open the dialogue in a way that demonstrates you have respect for the employee and make it clear that you are asking for respect in return. This means you can't start with "What the hell were you thinking?" Instead you might want to start with "I know you've been working hard on this project, however...."

☑ **Frame the conversation.** You don't want to meet with someone for the purpose of telling him he did a terrible job and you're really upset with him. You want all of your criticism to be constructive. The goal of the conversation is to determine what went wrong and find a way to prevent it from happening again in the future. Start the conversation by explaining it in that fashion—you will immediately alleviate your employee's fears and discomfort.

☑ **Plan your conversation in advance.** This is another classic example of how you must think before you talk. Before you sit down with an employee, consider what went wrong from your perspective. Make some notes to organize your thoughts. Consider ways to avoid the same problem in the future before you talk to the employee about the problem. When you do sit down to talk, you will already have thought through the conversation and be prepared to handle it in the best way possible.

☑ **Be specific.** Telling someone they really screwed up may make you feel better, but it isn't likely to provide future change. You must be able to point to particular steps or acts the employee took that were incorrect, not well-reasoned, poorly planned, or dangerous. Highlight actual events, tasks, or actions. Then offer concrete suggestions for how to change things in the future. A general admonishment to "do better next time" isn't helpful at all. Lay out the steps to success so that your employee can follow them easily. Help your employee see exactly what went wrong and rehearse strategies to avoid similar problems in the future.

☑ **Get him or her talking.** Ask the employee to explain what was wrong about the choices that he or she made before you offer your own list. Getting someone to work through this helps them understand what went wrong. Once you have discussed the mistake, then ask what the employee should do the next time a similar situation comes up. Asking him or her to think of solutions makes the situation more palatable and less dictatorial. It also makes it more likely that he or she will actually implement these changes and feel as if it was his or her idea and incentive to do so.

☑ **Take notes.** In some situations, it will be important for you to document the conversation for the employee's record (in which case you should discuss with your HR department exactly how to document this and what situations require a formal "write up" versus informal notes to the file). Even if this is unnecessary, you will want to take notes about what you and the employee have discussed and agreed upon for your own reference. This will be helpful for you to come back to if there is ever a question.

☑ **End on a positive.** You must always end these types of conversations on a positive or upbeat note. This doesn't mean offering effusive praise, but it does mean offering a sincere thank you. Ending the conversation with a plan for how the employee can turn things around is a positive ending as well. When the meeting is over, the employee should feel empowered to make changes and improve the situation, not chastised and scolded. It is also important that any discussion in which criticism is offered does not leave the employee with a feeling of hopelessness. There must be a plan to move forward.

After Hours Activities

Getting your team together after hours for activities and events can be a great way to promote team spirit, get to know each other, and bond. Many companies have softball or bowling teams that serve this purpose. These kinds of events are enjoyed by many people, but as a supervisor you should be aware that there are also many people who do not enjoy them. Participation must be voluntary, and no one should be made to feel obligated to participate. Employees who don't participate shouldn't feel left out. You should also ensure that these activities do not interfere with day-to-day work and are kept solely as after-hours events.

Motivate Your Employees

Motivation is one of those elusive things people are always seeking, but are not sure how to find. Motivation is an emotional reason to do something. To succeed and be productive, your employees must have motivation to do so. There are all sorts of motivational techniques you can employ as a manager. Pep talks, group events, threats, inspirational e-mails, and more are employed by many supervisors. The key to motivating a group of people is that you as the supervisor must first buy into the motivational technique. If you begin each meeting with a certain technique, but you personally don't feel this is helpful (or really believe it), no one else is going to either.

To an extent, all these techniques can work. However, the best way to motivate your workplace is to help each employee to be self-motivating. People who find their motivation from within are more likely to carry through. Self-motivation is always stronger than outside motivation you impose on people. And the problem with motivation techniques is that they never work for everyone. Tapping into self-motivation may also mean responding to desires for promotion, money, prestige, or accomplishment. It can also mean encouraging each employee to live up to his or her potential every day.

Essential ways to self-motivate your work force:

☑ **Provide challenges and opportunities for growth.** These are necessary to prevent stagnation. There's no reason for a person to stretch if he or she isn't given new and challenging tasks. As a manager, you should reinforce growth opportunities on a regular basis so that they are in the forefront of employee's minds.

☑ **Don't stop using outside motivation.** Although self-motivation is the most effective, outside motivation enforces and reaffirms self-motivation, making the drive even stronger. Often, outside motivation is needed to jumpstart self-motivation. Motivational techniques can bring a team together with a common cause and feel as if they are all together as one.

☑ **Key into what motivates each employee.** Different incentives and situations motivate different people. As a leader, you should provide a variety of outcomes that will match various employee approaches.

☑ **Don't assume everyone can self-motivate.** Not all of your workers are going to be able to rev themselves up and maintain their energy levels. But some will be able to, and you want those employees to be encouraged.

☑ **Use the company mission statement.** The company mission statement must be more than words on a wall for your employees. You need them to internalize it, believe in it, and seek to put it into practice every day. Point out examples that reinforce the motivating themes your company is organized around. If your motto is "Customer service, above and beyond," you should recognize and reward the employee who ran out into the parking lot with a package that a customer forgot as an example of the motto in action.

☑ **Don't assume motivation is stagnant.** Employees' motivation changes over time. Promotion may be a carrot for an employee at one point in his life and of no interest to him at another point. Be aware of the changes in motivation, and change your strategies to suit them.

Managing Difficult Employees

Managing difficult employees will be a true test of your ability to lead. It's easy to manage people whom you like and who make your job easy. Every workplace has some difficult employees whom you will need to learn to manage.

Identify the situations that create problems with certain employees and do what you can to avoid them. If your assistant always becomes argumentative when asked to clean up the conference room after a meeting, you might want to reconsider whether it is worth getting into it with her or if it might make more sense to delegate that task elsewhere. Your role is to prevent difficult employees from distracting you and your team. You must mitigate their effect on your team.

You will also need to identify which difficult employees provide a benefit to the company and which do not—and eventually fire those who do not. (See Chapter 4 for more information about firing employees). Before you do so though, evaluate the employee's overall value before giving up. It is possible to convert a problem employee to an asset with the right plan and the proper implementation.

When working with difficult people, your cardinal rule should be to always take the high road. Don't get involved in arguments, don't retaliate. You also must focus on what you can do to turn the employee around. What is at the heart of the behavior? Is it a personality conflict with someone else? Is it that he or she is not a good fit with his or her job requirements? Don't assume the employee is just a difficult person until you examine the situation from all angles.

The best way to turn a difficult employee around is to get him vested in the situation. If your customer service rep is always criticizing the way orders are fulfilled, give him an opportunity to present customer concerns to personnel and offer his suggestions for how to improve things. You could also consider a change in job responsibilities so that he is responsible for order fulfillment. It's easy to mouth off, but people get a lot quieter when they are given a functional role in fixing the problems.

Manage Non-standard Employees

If you have employees who use flex time or who job share, you may find that they are more difficult for you to manage.

Flex Time

When managing employees on flex time, first make sure you have a firm understanding of what the company policy on flex time is, or what the special arrangements are that have been worked out for this employee.

Get a firm schedule from the employee. Flex time does not mean you work whenever you feel like. It means you work at times off the regular clock. Follow up to make sure the employee is keeping to the agreed upon hours by checking log-ins, sign-in sheets, punch clocks, or by stopping in once in a while or calling.

Develop a good understanding of deadlines. If something is due by the end of work on Friday, make sure it is clear whether you mean the end of your work day or the end of the employee's work day.

Develop clear communication conduits. The employee must be available to interface with other employees, clients, vendors, and so on during regular business hours for at least part of the week. Set expectations for how quickly phone calls and e-mails will be answered.

Job Sharing

If you have employees who are sharing one job, it can be confusing to manage them effectively. If possible, have a meeting with both employees so that you can all talk about who is responsible for what and get a firm schedule down. Indicate if you need to be informed when they switch days or hours. Make it clear that even though they may divide the work up, they are both going to be responsible for meeting the job description for the position, and if one person drops the ball, the other will need to pick it up. Make sure the two people handling the job are a good fit. If they approach the job differently, there needs to be middle ground, and you must be sure they aren't duplicating work by each doing something in their own way.

Temp Workers

Temp workers are a great way to fill a short-term need or a part-time position. Choose an agency that understands your industry. Get details on their screening process so that you can feel comfortable with their selections. When you have a temp worker, treat him or her the same as you treat your other employees. Just because they are not permanent employees does not mean they are not as valuable or important as other team members. Be prepared to help a temp worker adjust to the learning curve that comes with the position. You will want to be sure the agency and worker understand confidentiality requirements, and you may want to limit temp workers so that they do not take work home because they may not come back the next day. Keep in mind that many temp workers turn into terrific permanent full-or part-time employees, so keep your eyes open for good workers.

Manage Out of the Office Employees

In your role as supervisor, you may have to manage employees in several geographic locations, telecommuters, freelancers, or outsourced workers. These types of employees present different challenges.

Telecommuters

Telecommuting can be a very effective way to keep valued employees happy and reduce your expenses, but it requires employees who have discipline and are able to get their work done outside of the office environment.

Essential steps to managing telecommuters:

☑ **Set clear goals, deadlines, and expectations.** Meeting these are the only way telecommuters can prove themselves to you.

☑ **Establish a trial period.** If telecommuting is new to your team or to this employee, agree that you will both try this arrangement for a period of time and then determine how well it is working. A defined review cycle will give you both the option of reevaluating the arrangement. For example, you don't want to eliminate the telecommuter's desk if he or she is going to end up back in the office in a month when the plan does not work.

☑ **Address problems immediately.** As soon as you are aware of a problem with a telecommuter's work, things are probably pretty far advanced, so you need to act as soon as possible to salvage the project, keep the client happy, and replace the person (if necessary).

☑ **Have pre-determined times when the employee is always reachable by phone.** This is important, particularly if other employees need to interface with the telecommuter.

☑ **Don't take advantage of your telecommuters.** Studies have shown that telecommuters tend to do more work than those in the office because they have fewer interruptions. Don't pile on more work because of this.

☑ **Keep an eye on expenses.** If your employee is being reimbursed for expenses, make sure you carefully review them.

Different Locations

If you are managing employees at two (or more) different locations, it may seem hard to stay on top of everything at once, particularly if one location is your home base where you spend the most time. To manage effectively, you need to know these essentials:

➡ Be visible at all your locations as much as possible. You want to be a familiar presence to employees and you also want to see firsthand the work that is happening there so you can evaluate it yourself.

➡ Don't visit other locations only when you are going to deliver bad news or reprimands. Show up with good news or no news at all so that your appearance doesn't trigger a negative response.

➡ Put a reliable person in charge at each location who can respond to things in your absence.

You need a right-hand man or woman in every location because you can't be everywhere at once. There needs to be a clear conduit for information to reach you, and clear authority in your absence.

■➤ Establish a schedule and stick to it so everyone knows where you will be. You need to be reachable and have a schedule that can be relied upon. However, make a point of showing up on a different day or a few hours early from time to time so that you catch employees when they are not expecting you.

■➤ Manage your time at each location. Have a plan for what you want to accomplish on your trips there. Make sure the necessary people are aware of it and are prepared. All prep work should be done before your appearance.

Freelancers

Freelancers and outsourced workers can augment your team capabilities and help you meet peak demands. To work effectively with these professionals, keep these essentials in mind:

■➤ Have a roster of people who are available and know their costs so that you don't have to scramble when you suddenly need help. If you are taking on a new freelancer, get references.

- Set deadlines and timetables so that expectations are clear.

- Set timetables up front and verify that the freelancer can complete projects within those constrictions.

- Have confidentiality agreements in place when necessary.

- If close interaction with your team is needed, have the freelancer work in your office for the duration of the project.

- Don't overlook overseas outsourcing as an option. This has become a popular and very affordable option for many companies.

Managing Managers

If you are managing other supervisors, keep in mind that they are your team members, but their team members are also part of your "extended family" as well. To effectively manage people who are in turn managing other people:

✓ Allow them to manage in their own style. Each manager is different and approaches things their own way. Give your managers the room to handle things, as long as they get results and are generally consistent with your own overall approach.

✓ Don't undercut their authority. If employees are to respect a manager, they must see that you do. Don't allow employees to bypass a manager and come to you. Direct all things that are within a manager's authority back to that manager.

✓ Establish a flow of information that is clear. Identify what kinds of information you need from your managers, how you expect to receive it, and how often you will need it.

✓ Create clear decision-making authority in your managers. Give them the power to make those decisions that are appropriate and don't step in and do it for them.

✓ Monitor them as you would any employee. Be sure they follow through with your initiatives and that their team completes all necessary work.

✓ Create standard operating procedures. Implementing these will direct your managers to follow your basic approach.

✓ Engage with all employees in the chain. Be friendly and get to know all the employees (to the extent possible) that your managers are in charge of.

Establish Accountability

When an employee works for an employer, he or she is accountable to them in some way. The company or employer that pays the salary, wages, or commission wants to make sure it is getting a good value. In order to prove this, employees must be successful at their jobs. You know that you are responsible to your own manager for the job or role your team is supposed to play. You need to establish the same kind of accountability between your employees and yourself.

In order for your team to fulfill its role, each employee who works under you must also be accountable and meet goals. All of your employees realize they work for you, but that is not the same as being accountable to you. They must feel as if their work is being evaluated by you. They need to see that you are monitoring what they do, but they do not need to feel as though you are breathing down their necks.

Essentials of establishing accountability:

☑ **Stay on top of things.** You must keep track of everything that is going on inside your department and have a sense as to how projects or responsibilities are progressing. It can be tempting to delegate tasks and wash your hands of them. As a manager, you need to keep your finger on the pulse of work that is happening. That does not mean you need to become involved in all the work, just that you need to keep yourself informed as to how things are going.

☑ **Be consistent.** If your workers know you are always going to read every page of a proposal, or that you will always double check contracts they prepare, they will always work to their highest potential. Important functions should be checked regularly. Lesser items can be spot-checked to ensure quality. When you check your employees' work, you send the message that you are watching and evaluating everything. You're letting them know that their work is important to you. To succeed, employees must meet your approval.

☑ **Be fair.** If you are nit-picky and always find fault with things, your employees will soon learn they cannot please you, so they will see no need to put extra effort into work. They will feel that they are overly accountable for everything. Instead, change the things that need to be changed and be willing to let the tiny details go by sometimes.

☑ **Admit your own mistakes.** If you present yourself as only human, your employees will feel much more comfortable having you evaluate their work. If you present yourself as God's gift to the company, they are likely to feel resentful of your oversight.

☑ **Set specific goals, timelines, and milestones.** It is much easier to be accountable if you know what you are accountable for and when. Imagine taking a calculus course that has no course schedule. You have no idea when the tests will be and no idea what material you should do for homework. There's simply no way to focus. But a class that provides you with a solid syllabus and a detailed calendar will allow you to relax because you know what you have to do when. You must do the same for your employees and make sure everything they need to know is spelled out for them in detail.

☑ **Hold employee reviews.** Employee reviews are one of the most important ways you can create accountability. In a perfect world, you should have two informal reviews and two formal reviews with each employee every year. In many situations, that is not realistic and the most you will be able to do is one formal review every six months or one every year. For more information on employee reviews, see Chapter 4.

Holiday Hassles

The winter holiday season is traditionally a time when many people slow down their productivity. They are busy thinking and talking about holiday plans, shopping during time off, shopping online, and being tired from festivities. Keeping up productivity at this time of year is a challenge.

As a supervisor, your role is to carefully watch output, track deadlines, and make sure work that must get done is completed on time during this time of year. You don't have to be a Scrooge, but someone has to keep an eye on the bottom line, and that person is you. It is also your responsibility to notice when you need to let things throttle back a bit. Many businesses slow down during the holidays, and yours may be one of them.

One challenge of the holiday season is employees taking time off. If you are in charge of granting requests, you need to be fair in making your decisions, but you also have to honor company policies and requirements. Making sure someone is in the office who can get urgent things done is important. Try to arrange time off requests so that productivity is impacted as little as possible. If you let both of your engineers take the same week off, you could encounter a serious problem and have no one to fix it.

Increase Productivity

No matter what kind of work your team does, you'll always look better to your supervisor if your team is able to increase the amount of work it does. It may seem like an impossible proposition to you. After all, you may think, everyone is already working eight hours a day, five days a week. How can you increase the amount of work without increasing the amount of time? The answer is, that as a supervisor, you should always be looking for ways that will allow your team to get more done in less time. You don't have to work your team into the ground to accomplish this.

Look for timewasters such as:

- Duplicative forms.

- Meetings that are too long or too frequent.

- Conference calls that involve unnecessary people.

- Procedures that create waiting times before more work can be done.

- E-mails copied to unnecessary people.

- Incomplete work that forces people to backtrack.

- People doing other people's jobs.

In addition to the company created timewasters, look for employee created timewasters as well:

- Too frequent smoking breaks.

- Long lunches.

- People coming in late or leaving early.

➡ Excessive small talk, gossip, or horseplay.

➡ Time spent on the internet for non-work-related things.

➡ Disorganization.

Creating procedures is an important way to boost productivity. You need to make sure that everyday procedures and processes are documented, so that if an employee calls in sick, goes on medical leave, or quits, there are instructions available for those who will be trying to pick up the slack. Many employees may not want to completely document their procedures because they feel not doing so gives them more job security—replacing them is then more difficult. As the supervisor, you must insist on what is best for the company, and that means having clear procedures in place.

A stumbling block to productivity as a manger is relying too much on one employee. Just as you can't run your department single-handedly, you also can't run it by just relying on one person. To improve productivity, everyone in the department must be an active and important member of the team who contributes to the work load.

Essential tips to help employees increase their productivity:

☑ **Try to keep work on an even keel.** There are a lot of teams that work at a leisurely pace and then are forced to kick things into serious overdrive as a deadline approaches. An ongoing pattern of working to the bone and then trying to recover from it is actually less productive than keeping things on a constant smooth level of even productivity. That doesn't mean there won't be a crisis from time to time. But a pattern of going from one crunch to the next is exhausting.

☑ **Set specific goals.** Setting specific goals and milestones gives employees something concrete to reach for. Simply telling them that they need to increase productivity is not specific enough.

☑ **Make changes to the status quo.** It's unlikely that productivity will change if nothing else changes. Realign your team, reassign responsibilities, set new goals, change procedures, and generally mix things up. Some changes will have an impact, while others don't. Over time you will learn what affects productivity within your department and you will be able to target changes more effectively.

☑ **Make it easy for them to do more.** Simplifying procedures, placing tools or supplies convenient to your workers, or taking away administrative tasks will free up employees to concentrate on productivity. It often makes sense to shift job responsibilities around so that similar responsibilities are given to one person. Instead of expecting all of your HR staff to manage payroll, assign it all to one person.

That person will be more focused and effective because she is the one person handling the whole ball of wax. Having several people do different parts of the same job can be confusing and will often end up taking more time because they have to coordinate with each other about who has done what.

☑ **Get feedback.** If your employees are not meeting the productivity levels you would like, find out why by asking them. They will likely be able to point out obstacles that are not evident to you. Some of them may be beyond your control, but it is likely that there will be some helpful information.

☑ **Get outside input.** Talking to other managers in your company, or reaching out to management associations within your industry, can open your eyes to productivity barriers you did not consider before.

☑ **Change the mentality.** Oftentimes a lack of productivity can be attributed to a lack of morale. Refer to the section in Chapter 1 about improving morale.

☑ **Plan for success.** Productivity commonly fails to live up to expectations because managers, employees, and companies do not plan for success. For example, if a new billboard ad is planned, make sure you have distribution in place for the product to meet potential demand. You can't wait and see what happens; you must have a plan in place that will allow you to achieve success before anything else happens.

Get Organized

A lack of organization is probably most responsible for a lack of productivity in any company. Disorganization creates more work for everyone. Encourage every single employee to have an organized workplace and to keep shared areas organized as well. Create a workplace initiative to inspire organization. This means that everyone needs to have a system, a plan, and a commitment to keep them going.

It may seem time consuming to have every employee do filing once every few days, but it is more time consuming and potentially damaging for the entire office to search for important documents that have disappeared before the big meeting.

As always with management, you must do what you say, so you have to set the example and be organized yourself. This means having a filing system that makes sense, designating in and outboxes, and having specific policies about what you will do with particular items. It also means knowing your calendar and following it, answering e-mail promptly, and returning phone calls within a reasonable amount of time.

Chapter 3

Communication Basics

Communication, whether verbal or nonverbal, is truly the key to your relationships with employees. Obviously, what you say and how you say it has a tremendous impact on how you relate to each other, how your employees feel about you, and whether you can build a team for success together. What is not so obvious is that there are many things you can do to improve your relationship and your employees' attitudes by making small adjustments in the way you communicate in the workplace. Communication is the most basic building block of a relationship. Paying attention to the communication you have with your employees can bring to light all kinds of problems and undercurrents, and can also help you discover and emphasize the positives. Working at how you communicate allows you to make small changes that have a great impact on the overall relationship.

How Your Communication Is Interpreted

To understand how what you say and do is interpreted, you must understand the lay of the land from your employees' point of view. You may mean one thing, while they interpret what you say or do in an entirely different way because of preexisting prejudices or experiences. For example, you may be rushing out to a meeting and tell an employee you don't have time to discuss the new billing format. She may interpret this as a brush-off, while you simply meant you were in a hurry and would find time to discuss it later. To make things work within your team, you have to develop sensitivity to how your words and actions are interpreted by others. This doesn't mean changing who you are, but it does mean trying to be more aware of the impact of your words.

Feedback

When you communicate, you must not only pay attention to what you're saying and how you're saying it, but also to how your communication is being received. Watch the body language and facial expression of the person you are speaking to. You will be able to pick up clues that indicate if the person is not understanding, uninterested, overwhelmed, and so on. You can then adjust the way you are communicating to further their understanding or increase their interest.

Implications

One of the basics of communication is that words are not interpreted simply by their literal meaning. Many things come into play when the meaning is understood, whether by body language, previous experience, environment, expectations, tone, phrasing, and so on.

You may say, "Could you please get me the Tanner file?" in lots of different ways, and someone listening could interpret it in lots of different ways, depending on your phrasing, emphasis, and their personal experiences:

- ➡ "Could you PLEASE get me the Tanner file?"

- ➡ "COULD you please get me the Tanner file?"

- ➡ "Could YOU please get me the Tanner file?"

- ➡ "Could you please get me the TANNER file?"

Each of these examples demonstrates an underlying message or implication. The first three indicate varying levels of annoyance. The last implies doubt about the ability to understand basic instructions.

Your tone of voice, facial expression, and emphasis affects the way the words are interpreted. Being aware of the many meanings words can have is a basic building block in understanding and improving your relationships with employees. Once you are attuned to the different things one set of words mean, you can try to deliver them in a way that sends the message you want them to receive.

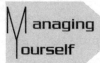

anaging

ourself

Results Through Wording

You want to get results from your employees; choosing your words carefully in your day-to-day communication at work can help you do that. Obviously there are many words that are not appropriate. However, there are other less obvious word choices to be careful with. Some managers get hung up and use the same words over and over. For example, a manager who always talks about whether things are in the company's "sweet spot" or who constantly urges employees to "hit the ground running" can get very annoying. You may not realize how often you use a certain word or phrase, and it can be helpful to ask your spouse or friends to point out things you're hung up on.

There are some industry words or management words that people can overuse. For example, some people prefer to use words such as "synergy" because they think it shows that they are very business-minded. Use words similar to this only when directly appropriate. Also, try to avoid using marketing language when talking to your employees. Don't call it an Ultra Fastening Device, even if that is what your company formally refers to it as, when it is really just a screw. Don't use specialized language you don't understand when talking to your employees, because you're likely to make a fool of yourself. If an employee uses a term you are unfamiliar with, either be honest at the time and ask what it means or do some checking and find out after the discussion so you are prepared the next time it comes up.

There are many other essential common words and phrases managers misuse or overuse:

I'm Sorry

Saying "I'm sorry" is an automatic gesture for some people and is a way of expressing empathy without accepting blame. If your assistant forgot a notepad in your office and came back to get it you might say "Oh, I'm sorry, there it is." You aren't saying you are accepting blame, but are saying you are sorry the inconvenience happened to him or her.

Other people hardly ever use the words "I'm sorry" because it means admitting fault or accepting blame. Some people mistakenly believe that using these words reduces their authority. Supervisors must convey that they are not too full of themselves and are human. A complete lack of these words in your office vocabulary can be just as much of a problem as overuse.

Examine your own speech patterns. Do you say "I'm sorry" too often? Do you rarely say it? Ask co-workers and friends and try to notice how often you use this phrase. Saying it too much is a symbol of inferiority. Not saying it enough may mean that you do not exude empathy. Find a good balance in your use of these words at work. Saying "I'm sorry" is an appropriate way to take ownership of problems. You want to express empathy, yet not accept blame for everything. For example, if you apologize for everything that goes wrong in the office, you're saying it too much. "I'm sorry it's so hot in here" or "I'm sorry the printer is jammed" are examples of excessive usage. But if you hand someone a work order and it drops on the floor before he takes it from you, saying "I'm sorry" is the right response. You should apologize for things that are your fault (even if they are accidents) that in some way make an employee's life more difficult. Whenever you say the words, you must be completely sincere about them. Using them too often will reveal a lack of sincerity that employees will pick up on. "I'm sorry" should never be used sarcastically by managers at work.

Learn to express empathy in other ways without saying "I'm sorry." Saying "Oh no! Are you okay?" when someone trips over the phone cord or "How awful! I hope he is better soon," when an employee describes his father's pneumonia are appropriate responses that don't imply any kind of blame.

Please

Do you use the word "please" when you ask for things? "Please hold my calls." "Could you please let accounting know of the change?" The type of emphasis you place on this simple word can drastically alter the meaning of your sentence. "*Please* hold my calls" has a very different meaning than if the word is not emphasized. Try to avoid emphasizing this word unless you are trying to send a message of annoyance. Using "please" is a good way to show respect in your conversations. "After lunch could you please stop in the mail room and look for that package I'm expecting?" or "Sherri, could you come in here, please?" are acceptable usages. Saying please too often can be viewed as a sign of insecurity. Be polite in your conversation, but avoid using this word constantly.

Okay

Many people end their sentences, requests or orders, by asking "okay?" "I want you to call headquarters, okay?" This speech pattern is a way to get verbal affirmation that the person you are talking to understands you and is on board with what you're asking. It's also a way to soften direct commands and make them more conversational. However, similar to the other speech patterns discussed in this section, it can be overused. If you end almost every request or direction with "okay?", you're sending the message that you're not sure of yourself and you're not certain of cooperation. Try to limit your usage of this question.

Thank You

Thank you is one of the phrases that needs to be part of your common office speech. Say "thanks" or "thank you" when someone does something you appreciate, does something well, or when you simply want to boost morale. Saying thank you each time someone hands you a file or e-mails you a document can get excessive, so try to limit it to once per task or situation. Say thank you in front of other people (such as other employees or clients), so that employees feels publicly appreciated. It is important that when you thank someone, you do it with sincerity.

Could You. . .

Some people find themselves asking their employees to do things, rather than directing them to do things. To achieve the balance you need in your office, you will find that you need to ask "could you" some of the time, while giving directions in other instances. If you find yourself asking your employees "could you" for *everything* you need them to do, you are communicating the message that you are not in charge or that you don't expect cooperation. By using the phrase "could you" on occasion, such as "Could you do the Brant letter first?" and "Before you send that to the client could you run it by me one last time?" you send the message that the employees have control over their work, and you are also conveying that you appreciate it when they do things that you ask. Make sure you intersperse your "could you's" with direct requests for urgent or important things when necessary. Much of the time, it is simpler and more straightforward to say "I need" or "I'd like you to" instead of "could you."

Common Courtesy

Some of the words we have described in the previous section are simply common courtesy. There's no reason to be stiff and formal with your employees, but it can be easy to let common courtesy slip away. Remembering to use words such as "please" and "thank you" can help keep the work place civil and comfortable. If you are ever unsure of how to handle a situation, using common courtesy will always be the right answer. Remember that the people who work for you are human and want to be treated with courtesy and respect. You can never go wrong by handling a situation with courtesy and politeness, so it should always be your fallback position.

Communication Pitfalls to Avoid

Obviously, when you are at work you are concentrating on getting your job done. You are not spending all your time thinking about your relationships with employees and how you communicate with them. No one who is successful in business has time to do that. However, there are some simple communication pitfalls to avoid that will dramatically improve the attitude and success of your office. Almost all of the no-nos can be rephrased to sound much better while conveying the same message. Learn to change some of these small simple things and you will find that your relationships will improve.

Essential rules for avoiding communication pitfalls:

☑ **Avoid saying anything that expresses disregard for employees' personal needs.** Instead of "I don't care if you have to pick your son up at four, this needs to be done now," say, "I just need you to stay for 10 more minutes, and I would really appreciate it."

☑ **Never belittle what an employee does.** Don't say "It's not that hard to get these invoices done and in the mail in a reasonable amount of time." Focus instead on the problem at hand: "Those invoices need to get into today's mail."

☑ **Don't express uncertainty in abilities.** Instead of "Do you think you know how to do this?" say, "If you have any problems figuring it out let me know."

☑ **Don't ignore the employee as a person**. It's easy to focus only on the work that needs to be done, but you do need to take time to talk to employees as people—ask what she did last night, where he went to lunch, where she got the new sweater, and so on. "So what did you do over the weekend?" or "Any luck selling your house?" are nice ways to relate.

☑ **Don't take out your annoyance on employees who are not responsible**. Scowling, slamming doors, or raising your voice creates a stressful office environment. It is okay to be upset, but taking these frustrations out on employees will cause resentment. If you find yourself in a foul mood (because after all, who doesn't from time to time?), don't feel as though you have to be sunny and cheerful, but do take the time to explain that you are in a bad mood, and try not to project your frustration with the problem onto your dealings with the people around you.

☑ **Don't lay your worries on your employees' shoulders**. While it's okay to talk sometimes about the challenges you face or problems that have come up, you can't be a leader if you reveal all of your weaknesses. Your employees are not your confidants. You shouldn't tell an employee about the fight you had with your husband or how you completely blew the last client meeting you had, but it is okay to share frustration about the problems with the construction on your home or talk about the embarrassing moment when you completely forgot the client's name.

☑ **Arrogance and superiority will get you nowhere with employees.** You really need them to like you as a person and want to help you succeed. You have to be human and you have to be approachable for this to happen. Avoid implying that you believe you are more intelligent, more important, or just better than he or she is. Don't be overly proud of your accomplishments in front of them. Have humility about what you do and how you deal with your success. At the same time, you must portray confidence and comfort with your work and decisions.

☑ **Avoid being condescending.** Sometimes, when an employee is acting like a child, it is very tempting and easy to talk to her as if he or she is a child. This kind of communication is not productive and only results in frustration and resentment. If you find yourself about to do this, just pause and take a breath before speaking so you can control what comes out of your mouth.

If You're Annoyed and You Know It Stamp Your Foot

While it's not okay to be consistently unpleasant, displaying a certain level of annoyance can be a helpful tool. When you are annoyed at something an employee or group of employees has done, showing your feelings can be a quick way to communicate your displeasure and get them to bring about change. You don't always have to sit down and seriously tell someone they have disappointed you. Making it clear through tone, body language, and word choice that you are displeased with something that has happened will get your employees' attention very quickly.

The caveat, of course, is that showing annoyance doesn't show employees the path to take next time or institute a path of improvement, so you want to be sure to have discussions when direction is needed. But when an employee has blown it and knows it, being ticked off can be motivation enough to get things turned around.

As with all behavior at work, as the manager, you are the one who sets the standard, so shouting, slamming things, or calling people names is not going to be effective. Stay within the bounds of courtesy.

Expressing Urgency

In business, there are often situations where something needs to be done NOW or where a problem comes up that needs to be worked on as soon as possible. Having your employees' whole-hearted help at these moments is indispensable, and is often the difference between getting something done and not getting the problem solved.

It is possible to express urgency or the need to get something done right away without stepping on toes, being dictatorial, or being unpleasant. Often during time crunches it is easy to let your annoyance, concern, and worry about the whole situation come out in what you say. If you find yourself doing this, take one deep breath before issuing your orders or instructions. You can be stressed out without snapping at people.

When something is urgent, it is often useful to tell your employee or employees why it is urgent. When you ask someone to drop something and finish something else quickly, explain to them for example, that your biggest client has asked for this; it makes the situation easier to understand. It is definitely true that because you are the manager you should be able to direct an employee to do something without explaining yourself, but most of the time if you can offer a brief explanation it will help the employee feel part of the situation and more vested in it. An explanation also shows that you respect the employee's work process.

Essential ways to express urgency in a way that will make employees want to help without resenting you include:

➡ "We're in a big time crunch here. I need you to...."

➡ "This needs to get to Todd Sanders' office by the end of the day. I know it's short notice but...."

➡ "I would really appreciate it if you could get to this first, before anything else this morning."

➡ "Hold onto your hat. We've got another one of those crises from the office in Chicago."

Suffusing appreciation, humor, or a casual feeling of being in this together takes the bite out of an urgent request and makes employees want to cooperate and get the job done as quickly as possible. When an urgent matter has been successfully completed, express your appreciation and let those involved know what a relief it was to have help in getting it done. "Thanks for the help on this one," "We never could have gotten this done without your help," and "I'm really pleased at how this project turned out. You did a great job," are ways to demonstrate your appreciation and smooth over any problems that may have resulted from an urgent or pressing situation where tensions can run high.

Offering Corrections

Some supervisors and managers find that it is hard to find the words to correct their employees. They don't want to offend them, seem as if they are on a power trip, or act like a perfectionist. Many people remember situations where they were criticized or corrected at work and want to avoid the discomfort they felt. There will be times when you will need to explain that an employee is doing or did something wrong. You don't want to do it to make him or her feel bad, but you don't want it to happen again. Mistakes hurt your business and succeeding in business is your ultimate goal. Learn to use corrections that get the job done without causing bad feelings.

Try these types of corrections:

- ➡ "Next time you do this, could you...."

- ➡ "I know you worked hard on this, but this isn't exactly what I had in mind. If you change x, y, and z we should be all set."

- ➡ "I'm sorry to have to ask you to do this over, but it's missing x and y."

- ➡ "Let's do this differently next time. Instead of x, how about we do y."

- ➡ "Hmm, this isn't what I meant. What I meant was...."

- ➡ "If something like this comes up again, next time you should...."

- ➡ "I need you to do ____ this way next time."

One way to offer corrections is to use "I" messages instead of "you" messages. Focus what you are saying on the way the problem has impacted you or how it has made you feel instead of focusing on him or her and what he/she has done wrong. Starting a sentence with "you" focuses the blame directly on him/her, whereas starting a sentence with "I" focuses the situation on you and is not accusatory.

Don't Say	Say
You did this wrong. The numbers go in the third column, not the first.	I think this is mixed up. The numbers go in the third column, not the first.
You don't answer the phone the right way. Say x instead of y.	I think it would sound better if you say x instead of y when you answer the phone.
You really need to straighten up these files. It's a mess in here.	I have a hard time working when things are disorganized. Could you get these files put away this morning?

It can also be helpful to use a message focused around a client. Saying "Most clients prefer to receive it this way..." is a good way to refocus an employee without placing blame and it also removes your own personal preferences from the mix and directs the employee's attention on what the client's needs are.

When I Was in Your Job...

As a supervisor, you have a certain level of experience, education, or skill that your company has recognized by placing you in your current position. Because of this, you may have the wisdom of your past experiences. These can be very helpful to your employees. Telling someone about how you solved a challenge when you were in their position can provide very helpful advice (and is usually much better received than simply telling someone how to do something). Talking about your experience can also demonstrate that you have empathy for what your employees are going through. If you started as a stock clerk or desk clerk and worked your way up, you have certainly been in the shoes of many of your employees and you understand their jobs, their frustrations, and their experiences.

Part of your role as a manager is not only to ensure that the work gets done, but that the people doing it are reasonably satisfied and comfortable. Sharing your own experiences will give your employees a level of comfort in knowing they are being managed by someone who truly has been in their shoes.

Body Language

What you say with your body and face speaks volumes. Improving the message your body sends out will improve your overall relationship with your employees. Use these essential tips for more effective body language:

- ➡ Smiling when you say good morning or good night will make a huge difference in the way your employees see you.

- ➡ Avoid putting your hands on your hips when giving instructions.

- ➡ Make eye contact when speaking.

- ➡ Although you may often be in situations where you are sitting and an employee is standing, avoid giving lengthy criticism this way—people feel like a child standing before the principal in this kind of situation.

- ➡ Instead of always having an employee come into your office to receive instructions or calling her on the phone, go to her desk once in a while.

- Look at your employee when he speaks to you.

- Do not turn your body away when an employee is speaking to you.

- Avoid crossing your arms when speaking to employees.

- Don't lean or sit on an employee desk or chair when an employee is using it.

- Don't stand uncomfortably close to people.

- Let employees see you relaxed—such as with your jacket off—once in a while (although taking off your shoes in the office is a definite no-no).

- Don't yawn or stretch when an employee is talking to you.

- Avoid appearing too casual and relaxed, such as putting your feet up or laying on the floor.

- Don't turn your back when an employee is speaking.

- Reach your hand out to take what a person is giving you when possible.

- Don't roll your eyes or make any kind of derogatory physical motions in the presence of other employees.

- Don't tap your foot, fidget, or tap your pen while an employee is talking.

- Try to have important discussions when you are sitting at eye level with each other.

Tie It All Together

Your words, body language, and tone should all send the same message when you are talking to an employee. It requires either complete honesty or careful control to align all three, but if you don't, you send mixed messages. Praising someone while frowning will not offer worthwhile feedback. Sometimes we unconsciously mix our messages because we're talking about one thing but thinking about something completely different that causes our body language to imply something other than the spoken message. It may take some concentration to make sure that you are sending one unified message, but the result will be better communication with your employees.

Setting a Tone

You can use the way you communicate to set the basic tone for your work place. If you make an effort to speak clearly, calmly, and in a friendly way as often as possible, you set a tone of cooperation, friendliness, and comfort. If you speak hurriedly, raise your voice occasionally, and make it clear through your speech that you are not happy, it will set a tone for your office that is stressful, pressured, and unpleasant. The more pleasant the work environment, the more happily your employees will do what you need.

Try to use a normal tone of voice when you speak to your team. A calm, friendly tone is the best way to ask for things or give instructions at the office. If you are always in a panic, spitting out rapid-fire orders, and speaking in a tight, tense tone, your team members will respond to your emotions and will become tense.

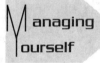

Managing
Yourself

Saying What You Mean

A communication problem is a failure to say what you mean. Some people imply what they mean, circle around it, and give clues. It is important to learn to be specific and clear about what you're saying and what you mean when speaking to your team members. You can't assume that the person you are talking to is getting what you are saying. Instead of saying "Can you do something with this PowerPoint presentation?" and assuming the employee will figure out what needs to be changed say, "Can you improve this PowerPoint presentation for me? It needs some calm background music, charts taken from the year-end report, and some kind of splashy border."

Effective communication is clear and concise. Your point should be easy to understand, and an employee should not have to think about what you said to get to the meaning. In order to achieve this, you have to know what you want, so try to make your message clear in your own head before you tell it to someone else.

Listening

One of the most important communication skills you can develop is the ability to listen. You need to listen not only to the words employees are using, but also to what they mean and how they feel. Tuning into the undercurrents in your office will clue you in to why work isn't getting done, why things take too long, and what exactly the source of dissatisfaction is. Learning to listen for what is really happening is the most proactive step you can take in dealing with employees.

Essential tips for effective listening:

☑ **Avoid prejudging what the employee is saying.** Don't assume you know what he is going to say or what he means before he says it. Don't form an opinion about what he is saying before you hear the entire statement.

☑ **Avoid selective listening.** Don't tune out things you don't want to hear or things you think you aren't interested in. You may miss important information or important emotional cues this way.

☑ **Pay attention to detail.** It is easy to focus on the big picture (for example, an employee's problem working with spreadsheets), when the details of what he is telling you reveal specific issues or problems that can be dealt with (a misunderstanding about which items go into which column, which you can easily clear up).

☑ **Look interested.** Look at your employees when they talk, instead of shuffling papers or making notes in a file. People talk more to a person who seems interested in what they are saying.

☑ **Agree to listen only when you have time.** If you don't have time at that moment or cannot focus, ask to have the conversation another time. No employee wants to talk to a boss who is distracted.

☑ **Read body language.** Pick up on the nonverbal cues that accompany employee words and respond to them in appropriate ways, such as keeping a disinterested employee interested during a meeting.

☑ **Display open, interested body language.** Crossing your arms or swinging your leg will indicate boredom or annoyance and make it clear you are not interested in what he or she is saying.

☑ **Respond appropriately.** Answer questions or statements with words and complete thoughts instead of "mmm-hmm" or "uh-uh."

It is also important to recognize when an employee is not telling you the full story. It is really easy for someone to just say things are good when you ask how a job is going, when in fact there are problems. Keep your eyes and ears open for people who are telling you what they think you want to hear. If you think this is happening, ask questions that will get more details and more information so you can get to the truth.

Essential Written Communication:

In addition to listening to your own employees, you also need to learn to listen to other employees. Be aware of conversations in the hall, elevator, lunch room, and so on. These conversations can give you information about what is going on in your own team as well as in the company in general.

117

There are certain things that you must have in writing in order for your team to work effectively:

- Deadlines.

- Employee expectations.

- Job descriptions and responsibilities.

- Standard operating procedures.

- Emergency contact information. (Who to go to for specific things.)

- Project plans.

- Records of client communications.

- Employee reviews and disciplinary actions.

- Formal requests for things such as time off.

Effectively Using Different Vehicles for Communication

We all use a variety of communication media to get business done. E-mail, voice mail, memos, reports, phone conferences, and more are important parts of your everyday work. Managing these different types of communication will improve your effectiveness as a supervisor. You should make clear your expectations about what types of communication should be used at what times to your employees. Make it known that you would rather get something in an e-mail than in passing in the hallway or in a hard copy memo.

Essential tips for e-mail in the workplace:

You can also set expectations for how you expect employees to interact with each other with various kinds of communication vehicles.

E-mail

E-mail can be an effective tool, but it can also cause a lot of problems. Learning how to use e-mail effectively will help you and your team be more productive.

☑ **Use descriptive subject lines.** Failing to put in an accurate subject line makes it more likely that an e-mail will get lost or ignored. You should have a standard team policy that when an e-mail concerns a certain client or a certain project that it is identified in the subject line. And it should always be referred to in the same way so that it can be found by the search feature of your e-mail program. For example, if you are referring to Blue Flower Productions, don't abbreviate it as BFP or Blue. Also, it may be helpful to set up a system for your team in which e-mails about certain topics or functions are always labeled in a particular way, such as "payroll," "request for time estimate," and so on.

☑ **Set up folders in your inbox.** Create different folders for different things in your inbox and use the message rules to direct emails to these boxes. This will make it easy to find e-mails you receive and keep them organized and together.

☑ **Delete e-mail.** If you don't need it or have done whatever you need to do with an e-mail, delete it. If not, you'll end up with an inbox filled with thousands of e-mails.

☑ **Answer promptly.** E-mails are meant to be fast and immediate. If you let an e-mail sit, you're likely to forget about it, unless you are diligent about marking things as unread if you need to do further work on them. Failing to promptly answer e-mail from employees sends a message that you are not on top of things. You need to make a personal commitment to respond to e-mail in a timely manner and make it clear you expect the same of your employees. If you are unable to respond to the e-mail immediately, send an e-mail saying you got it and you will respond by such a date or time. This way you won't get three more emails asking if you got it and what the status is. Create a policy for your team and e-mail responses as well, asking that they be responded to within a certain period of time.

☑ **Don't forward junk e-mails.** We all get the occasional joke via email, but if you start sending these e-mails out to employees, it gives them license to do the same thing. Soon productivity will be reduced. If your employees send junk e-mails, create a policy that asks that they avoid doing so because it detracts from work time.

☑ **Only CC (carbon copy) or BCC (blind carbon copy) when necessary.** Some people get into the habit of CC-ing (copying in a way that lists all the people who have been copied) everyone in the department on their e-mails. All this does is clutter up inboxes and make it more difficult for people to find things and know which things they personally need to deal with. Only CC someone if it is necessary. BCC-ing (blind carbon copying) is copying someone on an e-mail in a way that does not allow the recipient to see you have copied this person) should be used only on rare occasions. Instruct your employees to do the same.

☑ **Set up groups.** If you regularly send e-mails to the entire team or to a group of people within the team, set up groups in your e-mail program so that you can type in the group name instead of all 17 individual names. Suggest that your employees do the same. You may wish to encourage people to create the same groups.

☑ **Pause before sending.** It can be very easy to fire off e-mail in the heat of the moment. In general, if you're upset about something, it is better to save the e-mail as a draft and think about it for a while before sending it. You might also want to set up your e-mail program so that there is a delay on sending things. Sometimes you hit send and suddenly realize something you should have said. If there's a delay, you can go into your outbox and make the change before the e-mail goes out.

Phone Calls

Effective use of the phone is an important skill all managers need to have. Treat a phone call similar to a face-to-face meeting. Speak as politely as you would in person and don't do other things while you are on a call. When you are talking on the phone, try to smile. It changes your voice and makes you sound friendlier.

Essential tips for phone calls:

☑ **Conference calls.** Have everything you need in place before you begin a conference call, and encourage employees to do the same. If you will not be speaking, put your phone on mute and direct employees to do this as well, because it cuts down on ambient noise. If you will be speaking, know who is on the call, take notes as you listen, and have your points ready to present.

☑ **Leaving voice mail.** Always identify yourself, even if you think the employee should know who you are. Although most voice-mail programs have date and time stamps, it can be helpful to leave that information if you don't think it is being provided. Voice-mail messages should be short and to the point. Try not to ramble. It is always helpful say why you are calling, rather than just asking the person to call you back with no explanation. It is helpful to think about what you want to say in advance so that if you get voice mail you'll know what you want to say. If you're taken by surprise by voice mail, it's okay to hang up and call back if necessary, but try to do it before the beep. If your office system allows you to listen to the message you've just left, you may wish to do so and re-record it if you are not happy with it.

☑ **Creating outgoing voice mail.** When you create the outgoing voice-mail message on your own phone, be sure you identify yourself. It is a good idea to record a new message when you go on vacation or are out of the office for a day or two so that people are aware of the delay in response. But make sure you change the message when you get back so people who call on June 20 don't get a message that says "I'll be out of the office on June 16." An option you may want to consider is recording a new voice-mail message each day with the date. This is a signal to people that you check your voice mail and keep it up to date. You can never go wrong leaving a simple, professional message, but a funny or quirky voice mail can backfire. You may wish to create a team policy about what information employees need to leave on their outgoing message.

☑ **Cell phones.** If your cell phone is a company expense, you should encourage employees to call you on the office phone when possible and not the cell, to reduce costs. The same policy should apply to calls among employees.

Letters, Notes, and Memos

Letters, notes, and memos are becoming more infrequent with the increased use of e-mail, but are still important forms of communication. Always proofread written letters or memos before sending them out, to avoid embarrassing mistakes. Keep memos short and to the point. Set off or bullet point important information such as dates, figures, and important facts. Use memos sparingly, so that they signify something important and people pay attention to them. To cut down on memos, try answering some memos you receive with phone calls or meetings. Memos can be self-perpetuating. If you stop the cycle, you will reduce the paperwork for everyone.

Some people feel uncomfortable communicating in writing, particularly on a piece of actual paper (e-mail feels more informal and isn't as intimidating somehow). If you find yourself stumped about what to say when writing a memo or letter, think of what you would say if the person you are writing to were standing in front of you. Say it in your head and then transcribe it. Too often, people try to become very formal and stiff when writing letters. Keep it simple and worry about conveying your information, not about sounding like a great writer.

When you write notes, make sure your handwriting is legible. You don't want an employee to have to spend time deciphering it or having to call you to ask what it says. If your handwriting is simply bad, consider putting on the sticky note "see e-mail" and then send instructions or details by e-mail.

Reports

Writing reports can be time-consuming and may seem overwhelming. The first thing to do is look at a similar report so that you understand the format you need to follow and the information you need to include. Set up a template on your computer if you don't already have one, so that the sections of the report will be laid out for you. Opening a document and having something on the screen makes getting started a whole lot easier. If your company does not already use this format, it makes sense to attach a cover sheet to the report that summarizes the key information. This cover sheet will highlight the important points; the details will be provided in the report itself.

Organize all the information you need to include and outline it if necessary. It is much easier to start writing when you've got all the facts you need in front of you. You should always have a goal, purpose, or theme to the report; for example, the report may be tracking or identifying a product, work flow, or profit. Write the report with this theme in mind, so that everything in the report points to that general idea.

In some companies, reports can become excessive. As the supervisor, you may find that you're inundated with reports from employees. To reduce the amount of reports you have to weed through:

- ➡ **Look for duplication.** The same information may be reported to you in different ways. Try to reduce overlap so you only need to look at each piece of information once. This saves you time and increases your employees' productivity.

- ➡ **Look for automation.** There may be ways for your employees to have certain pieces of information generated by computers. Instead of spending a day compiling sales figures, a good computer program can provide this information at the touch of a button.

- ➡ **Lengthen reporting periods.** Instead of getting a report on employee overtime once a week, change it so you get it only once every month.

- ➡ **Restructure the actual reports.** Make them shorter. Reduce repetition within the reports themselves. Simplify them so they are in English, not techno-speak.

- ➡ **Substitute with meetings.** Holding a meeting to discuss the implementation of new safety procedures may be less time-consuming than having someone generate a report, circulate it, and then having to call for clarification. Sit down with all the information and talk through it. It may be helpful to produce notes from the meeting so that you have documentation.

Let Me Repeat Myself

When you are giving commands and instruction to others, repetition is an important tool. When you first direct someone to do something new, it is likely that their brain may not completely process all aspects of the task. In general, when you explain something new you need to offer a full explanation then ask if they have any questions. You can then summarize the task or job again briefly.

Sometimes when you are explaining something that is complicated, changing a long-standing procedure, or talking to an employee who is just not getting it, you may need to offer two full explanations. Saying the same thing over and over again is not helpful and can be insulting. Rephrase your instructions the second time. Using different words the second time can help the employee understand the instructions better. If you have any doubts about how well the employee understood you, ask him or her to explain to you what is expected. Having to put it in their words ensures they understand it and also helps them remember the details better.

It can also be helpful to use e-mail to repeat something. E-mail provides a firm record of a conversation and recording the details makes it clear what was discussed and offers a reference point if there is any question.

Foster Communication in Your Workplace

Becoming a good communicator is important, but you also must create an environment in which employees are encouraged to communicate well with you and with each other.

Essential ways to build good team communication:

- ☑ **Encourage listening skills.** Encourage people to stop and listen to each other, whether in a meeting, in a conference call, or face to face. Simply allowing people to complete their thoughts before someone else interrupts can support good communication.

- ☑ **Require respect.** If you create a work environment where employees respect each other, they will be able to communicate more effectively.

☑ **Create procedures.** Set ground rules for when employees should use e-mail, memos, face-to-face meetings, and phone calls with you and with each other. An employee who sends you 30 e-mails a day is not being helpful. Encourage employees to streamline their communications. Have a standard form that people use when taking phone messages for others and make sure they fill in all fields.

☑ **Create communication vehicles.** Set up systems that provide avenues for employees to share important information. Setting up a shared calendar on the team intranet can make it easy for people to schedule jobs and meetings. A client contact database can allow employees to record contact with clients so that the next employee involved can see exactly what happened and when the last contact was made.

Meetings

When you mention meetings, a lot of people groan. Very few people like meetings. Who hasn't spent valuable time in a meeting where nothing got accomplished and other work was waiting back on your desktop? Meetings don't have to be inefficient, annoying, and boring. As a supervisor, you'll probably be running meetings for your team, so it is up to you to set the tone for how meetings will be perceived by your employees.

Some people have strong opinions about meetings, such as limit them to a certain time period, follow tight procedures so it doesn't run out of control, and so on. The key to keeping a meeting bearable is to be in charge and help your employees see the benefits from the meeting. Use these essential suggestions:

➡ **When you start a meeting, start it.** Have a formal beginning to the meeting when all conversation stops and you have everyone's attention. Do not discuss meeting-related business as you're sitting around waiting for everyone to arrive. You'll just end up having to recap it all later. Do not tolerate tardiness—this must start with your own timeliness.

➡ **Begin on a positive note.** When possible, start each meeting with something positive or good. You may wish to recognize employee or team achievement or share a story of another kind of success. Get people feeling good at the beginning of the meeting and they will carry that positive energy forward throughout the rest of the meeting.

➡ **Make sure the agenda is clear.** There should be no question about what you're going to discuss. This will enable people to come prepared to the meeting and will allow you to organize what you want to accomplish. Encourage employees to submit topics for the agenda in advance of the meeting. Circulate the agenda prior to the meeting so that everyone knows what will be discussed and is prepared when they get there.

➡ **Hold it in a large enough space.** Make sure everyone can fit in the room and sit. If the room is too small, move the meeting outside or to a hallway or lunchroom.

➡ **Schedule it conveniently.** It can be hard to find a time when every member of your team can come to a meeting, but it makes sense to try to schedule it at a time that is most convenient for the most people. If you schedule a meeting before lunch or before the end of the day, you can be sure it won't drag on forever because people will be anxious to leave. However, if the meeting ends up going over, you'll have a bunch of hungry or impatient employees on your hands.

➡ **Don't make it mandatory unless it is.** Too many teams and companies schedule "mandatory meetings" for all team members or company members, then proceed to discuss things that do not apply to everyone there. Only those people who need to be at the meeting should be required to be there.

- **Be aware of length.** Set the length of the meeting in the agenda so that people can plan around the meeting. If something comes up, it may be necessary to extend the meeting, but first check to see if anyone will need to leave. If so, change the order of the agenda so that the most important items are handled first.

- **Make it fun.** This isn't always possible, but running boring PowerPoint presentations and going over figures that everyone has in front of them is not going to excite anyone. A meeting is not about hearing your own voice. Once in a while, plan something a little different for your meeting. Some managers prefer to read short inspirational stories, show brief film clips, play songs, or create mottos. Providing food is another way to keep people awake and make the meeting more enjoyable for everyone.

- **Encourage participation.** A team meeting involves the team. Allow everyone to have a voice and a role when possible. Employees who are allowed to give input into things become vested in them and work harder for their success.

- **Document the meeting.** Have someone take notes, so that there is a record of what was discussed or decided.

- ➡ **Be the leader.** If it's your meeting, you are in charge of what you're discussing, who is talking, and what is being resolved. Don't let the meeting run away from you. It's very easy to allow people to speak up with too many other questions or concerns and watch your meeting become completely derailed. Focus your meeting on the subject at hand and insist that other topics wait. Set the tone and pace of the meeting and carry it through.

- ➡ **Restate the action items at the end.** When you're wrapping up a meeting, repeat who is going to be doing what. Reiterate the deadlines for these responsibilities as well. Make certain that everyone understands what is expected of them and what the plan is.

One important factor to keep in mind is that meetings are costly. They take up people's time when they could be doing other productive work. For this reason, you should use meetings sparingly. There are times when a group e-mail or memo will suffice in place of a meeting. Use those opportunities when they are possible.

Some teams benefit from having regular meetings, such as once a week. This type of regular meeting allows for everyone to bring their questions and problems to one meeting, instead of coming to you at different times during the week. It also provides a regular life cycle of one week for questions to be answered or problems to be rectified, which can be a good incentive to keep things moving along. However, regular weekly meetings are not useful if things do not change quickly enough in your business for there to be enough to discuss each week. If there is nothing to discuss or work on, cancel the meeting. Don't have a meeting just for the sake of having a meeting, or worse, have everyone assemble only to be told you're not holding the meeting. Some teams begin regular meetings when a new team member is hired and slowly taper off, then when another new employee is hired, the meetings start again. You've got to be consistent with regular meetings. Find a length of time between meetings that is a good fit for your team and then stick to this schedule.

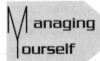

Managing Yourself

Communicating With Your Boss

Communicating with your own boss can sometimes be as problematic as communicating with your employees. The key to remember in communicating with your supervisor is that you want to convey respect.

Essential tips for better communication with your supervisor:

☑ **Understand what he or she wants from you.** Understanding what kind of information your boss expects in each conversation can help you prepare better for your conversations.

☑ **Look at him or her.** When you talk to your supervisor, be sure to make eye contact. However, because you are the subordinate person in the situation, you should not hold eye contact the entire time and should at times look away.

☑ **Be succinct but not abrupt.** Your supervisor's time is valuable and you need to respect that. Try to communicate what he or she needs to know without taking up too much time.

☑ **Wait until he or she has time.** Conversations with your boss should happen when he or she is not crunched for time. You want his or her full consideration and you don't want to squeeze what you have to say into too short a time period.

☑ **Be honest.** It can be tempting to keep bad news from your boss or try to downplay situations, but it is always best to be up front and clear with him or her because otherwise it will catch up with you later.

☑ **Don't share everything.** Your role is not to tell your boss everything, only to communicate those key pieces of information he or she needs. Think of what you want from your own employees, and provide that kind of focus when talking to your own supervisor. Over time you will learn what your boss finds to be important and you can tailor your communication in that way. Limit the number of memos you send to your boss, so that those you do send receive attention.

☑ **Keep it simple.** You want to impress your boss, but making things more complicated than they already are won't get you anywhere. Offer simple, clear explanations and information so that your boss knows you can be relied upon to be straightforward.

☑ **Respond promptly.** When your supervisor sends a memo, e-mails, calls you, or asks you something in person, respond as soon as possible. Complete the task or research the question thoroughly, but then get back to him or her about it as soon as possible.

When you do talk with your boss, you should not always be presenting problems or concerns. You want your boss to see you as someone who creates and presents solutions. Become that person. When you have to go to your supervisor with a problem, bring a solution if you can. If you aren't sure how to solve the problem, at least come to the meeting with several possible solutions so that you aren't walking out the door empty handed.

Chapter 4

Employment Issues

For many people, managing employees and projects are the fun part of being a supervisor. But dealing with legal and administrative employment issues is another important component of a supervisor's role. In your department, you are the legal head and must concern yourself with things such as discrimination, hiring practices, terminations, discipline, and privacy.

Job Postings and Resumes

Building a good team means hiring good people. As a supervisor, part of your responsibility is to hire people for your department. Hiring an employee is a significant investment of your time and money, so you want to go about it carefully and in a way that obtains the optimum results.

Finding good people can sometimes be challenging. Before you seek to hire a new person, first evaluate the resources within your own team. There may already be someone on the team who would be well-suited to move up to this open position. Promoting from within allows you to place someone in the job who needs less training than a person from outside the company. This saves you time and resources. You can then hire someone to fill that person's open position, which may take less training. Additionally, your company may require posting the job internally first before opening it up to outsiders, so you may have no choice but to consider existing employees for the position first.

Promoting From Within

When you promote from within, you hire someone who can probably make an easier transition into the job than if you hired someone new. However, when an employee makes the transition within your company or within your team to a new position, there are often some adjustments to cope with. Everyone on the team needs to understand what the person's new responsibilities are and not rely on them to solve things related to the previous position. Employees may also need to learn to respect someone who has been promoted above them. Make it clear what the newly-promoted person will be handling and what role he or she will play within the team.

The employee who is being promoted may need training to take on the new job and should be given some time to adjust to the new responsibilities and routine.

Essential first steps for hiring:

☑ **Create a clear job description.** Make a list of all the responsibilities this person will need to handle, if one is not already in place. Then translate these tasks into the skills necessary to complete them and include these in your description. Include information about specific requirements, such as generating a specific number of sales per month. If this is a new position that is being created, choose a name for the position that accurately reflects it. If someone else previously held this position, think about what skills they had that were necessary and what skills they were lacking to help you isolate the important needed skills.

☑ **Find out what you can offer in terms of salary or pay.** Get a clear salary or hourly range from your supervisor or company. Research what that position pays in your area and in your industry. You can also find online benchmarks for salary amounts. If you have discretion with this, you need to look closely at your budget and establish in your mind what your initial offer will be and how high you will go to get someone you really want.

☑ **Write a clear ad or job posting.** A job posting is shorter than a job description and is designed to accurately express the general gist of the position, enticing those who are qualified to apply. Don't get too creative with how you describe the job. You really want people to understand what it is so that only those truly interested will apply.

☑ **Get the job posting out to as many places as possible.** To get the best crop of candidates, you need to get your job listing in front of as many people as possible. Post it on Websites and take out ads in industry publications or local business publications. Put up a notice in the community area of your workplace because employees may know other people who would qualify. Talk to other managers within your company and other colleagues within your industry to find out if they know people who might be qualified. Word of mouth is a powerful tool. If the position is a highly-competitive one, you may find that using a headhunter will make the job search easier.

☑ **Check the files.** Your company or your predecessor may have applications on file from people who responded to previous openings or who submitted them cold. Consider applications or resumes that are no more than six months old. Place resumes and applications you receive into a file, but do not use this same file for future use.

Weeding through resumes or applications can be difficult. Look for people who:

- Clearly meet the qualifications.
- Instill confidence.
- Have relevant experience and education.
- Have solid work histories.
- Follow instructions and provide neat paperwork.

If possible create at least three tiers of applicants:

1. People you definitely want to interview
2. People you would consider if none of the top tier pan out.
3. People you are not interested in.

Note that it is simply good business practice to send an e-mail or letter to the people who applied whom you will not be considering, thanking them for their resume or application. If you set this up as standard practice, so that you or your assistant always do this, you won't have to deal with phone calls from people who want to make sure you got their application or resume or asking if you've made a decision yet. If you accept applications via e-mail, set up a separate address and an auto-responder to automatically thank people for their applications and tell them you will be in touch if you are interested, and to ask that they not call.

Once you have hired someone, keep the applications you were considering on file. The person you hire may not work out, and, you won't have to start from scratch to find a replacement.

Interviewing

An interview is the best way to evaluate a job candidate. When interviewing candidates you have two roles: On the one hand, you are the buyer. You are the one who is hiring—the interviewee needs to convince you to hire him or her. You job is to select the one candidate who is best for the position, so this means comparison shopping. You have to ask the hard questions, understand people's motivations, and be able to see through the buildup to the real person beneath.

On the other hand, you are selling the job to the candidate. You want to portray the position as one that he or she will want to do. As part of this, you should offer broad overviews of the company and details of the position. However, don't overstate the good aspects of the job—try to offer an honest portrayal. When you interview, be honest but not candid. Don't offer information that could be used by your competitors.

Essential first interview basics:

☑ **Come prepared.** Read the resume and/or application before the interview. Not doing so is just as unprofessional and annoying as a doctor who doesn't look at your chart before walking in the exam room.

☑ **Ask the right questions.** Many interviewers ask applicants why they're leaving their last job or why they want to work for this company. These questions usually offer nebulous answers. Instead, try asking what about this job appeals to the candidates and why they think they will be good at this. To learn about the last job, ask what about the last job did not appeal to the candidates or how it was not a good fit. It's also helpful to ask what the applicants know about this job.

☑ **Ask the same questions.** Asking all applicants the same questions will give you a good comparison point. How they answer the questions can be as revealing as their answers, so be sure to pay attention to that as well.

☑ **Discuss qualifications first.** If you begin an interview by talking about the job, it is easy for applicants to skew their skills and experience so that they appear to fit the description you just offered. Instead, start with their qualifications, then discuss the job.

☑ **Ask questions that require real answers.** If you ask, "Have you worked with engineering departments before?", you may get a yes or no answer. Instead, ask, "How have you worked with engineering departments in the past?" so that you get an answer with details.

☑ **Ask questions based on the application.** It's always a good idea to ask at least one or two questions about information on an application or resume. Not only will this help you verify that the information is true, but it will also give you the opportunity to talk about the applicant's past jobs and experiences, which can be very eye-opening.

☑ **Ask for examples.** Seek real examples of the applicant using skills or qualifications. Some questions might be examples of his most difficult challenge and how he faced it, her greatest success and how she achieved it, or his biggest failure and how he coped with it.

☑ **Identify gaps.** Ask about periods of unemployment to determine what happened. There may be an explanation such as an illness or personal situation. Be aware that self-employment may be a veil for unemployment, so get details about it.

☑ **Get references.** Always request references and always call them. Ask why the person left that job, how he or she performed, and if the person you are speaking to would recommend you hire him or her.

☑ **Keep money talk general.** You don't want to give an exact pay amount in your first interview, however it is a good idea to make sure the candidate understands the pay range the job is in, because it is a waste of everyone's time if the pay is too low for the candidate.

After you've done your first round of interviews, you will be able to narrow the field to your finalists—two or three is a good number. Interview these people again, ask harder questions, and pose possible scenarios. It is also a good idea to have another supervisor briefly interview the candidates as well so that you can get another perspective on the people, their personalities, and qualifications.

Once you are prepared to offer the job to one candidate you should prepare a formal job offer that includes details about pay, benefits, vacation, job duties, and so on. It is becoming more common for the candidate to counter-offer, and you will need to decide if you are willing to negotiate the terms you have offered or not.

Legal Hiring Requirements

You also must be aware of the legal restrictions on you when you are hiring employees. You cannot discriminate on the basis of:

➡ **Age.** The Age Discrimination in Employment Act of 1967 protects individuals over age 40 from age discrimination. This applies to employers with 20 or more employees.

➡ **Sex, Race, Color, National Origin, and Religion.** Title VII of the Civil Rights Act of 1964 prohibits discrimination against workers for any of these reasons. This law applies to employers with more than 15 employees. The Equal Pay Act of 1963 requires that men and women receive the same pay for the same work.

➡ **Disability.** The Americans With Disabilities Act makes it illegal to discriminate on the basis of a disability. However, you are permitted to tell employees about physical or mental requirements of a job, as long as you tell all applicants. Employers are required to make "reasonable accommodations" to allow disabled workers to do a job, as long as it would not impose an "undue hardship" on the company. This law applies to employers with 15 or more employees.

➡ **Pregnancy.** The Pregnancy Discrimination Act prohibits employers from making employment decisions based on pregnancy. This law applies to companies with 15 or more employees.

Note that these laws apply not only to the hiring of employees, but also to decisions involving pay, benefits, promotion, termination, and job responsibilities.

Sexual Harassment

Sexual harassment is a real problem in places of employment and happens when gender negatively impacts a person's job. This type of behavior violates the federal Title VII of the Civil Rights Act of 1964. The prohibited behavior includes unwelcome sexual advances, requests for sexual favors, and verbal or physical behavior that is sexual and interferes with work performance or creates a hostile or offensive work environment.

Sexual harassment is determined by looking at the whole situation, including the circumstances, the nature of the sexual advances, and the actual context. There are instances in which sexual harassment seems clear, such as requiring sexual favors to keep a job or making jokes about certain parts of a coworker's anatomy. But there are other instances in which it is a more subtle problem. For example, when a group of all male employees who are alone make sexual jokes about women or talk about coworkers in a sexual derogatory way, even if no female workers hears them, this is still inappropriate behavior because it creates a hostile environment (permitting employees to talk or act in a way that would be threatening or disruptive to others). There are men who are offended or insulted by this kind of talk as well. Just because all the people in the room are one sex does not make it acceptable to make comments or jokes about people of the other sex. Another subtle form of discrimination occurs when it is assumed that because a woman has children that she will not be able to work as hard or as well as men do. Some people also assume that everyone in a room is heterosexual when that is often not the case.

Getting Touchy

Touching can be a difficult category of sexual harassment and inappropriate behavior. There is some touching in the work place that is acceptable, such as shaking someone's hand or giving a pat on the back. In addition, women colleagues may touch more than men do. A rule that all touching is prohibited is not reasonable. Instead, the rule has to be that only appropriate touching is acceptable. As a supervisor, you should try not to touch employees unless it is a clear cut situation such as a handshake. Touching that might be appropriate between equals may not be appropriate when there is a power imbalance, so when there is a question, refrain from touching. Remember, you set the tone for what is appropriate in your workplace.

As the supervisor in your department, you are responsible for preventing sexual harassment, and dealing with it should it occur. This means that you must set the expectation that it will not occur and will not be tolerated if it should occur. A basic policy that the workplace has to be free of sexual jokes (this includes forwarded e-mails) and sexual comments can go a long way toward preventing any problems. Many people think they behave in an appropriate way, when in fact they make sexual comments or jokes from time to time with coworkers. In addition, there are also common instances where supervisors say "I know I shouldn't say this, but" or "Don't tell the HR department I said this, but." Even when you are in a one-to-one environment with an employee whom you feel will appreciate a joke or a comment, you have to suppress it. It takes a lot of care and attention to detail to prevent the appearance of sexual harassment, but it is absolutely necessary. Your rule of thumb should be to discourage any language or behavior that could possibly make anyone uncomfortable. You don't want to get into a situation where you try to determine if behavior falls under the legal definition of sexual harassment—you want to stop things well before they reach this threshold.

There must be a clear grievance or complaint process in place to deal with this type of problem, and if one does not exist in your company, you need to have a serious talk with your human resources department.

When you witness an inappropriate comment or action, it is your role as the manager to correct it. An egregious act requires a serious reprimand (and probably formal disciplinary action). But what do you do about small minor slips? After all, your employees are human. A small mistake is probably not a reason to embarrass an employee in front of others and may not call for a private talk, but you might want to send out a blanket e-mail simply reminding everyone of what the policy is and asking them to give their best effort in honoring the rule.

If there is an individual who was the recipient of a comment or could have been insulted by it, you must make sure he or she is not upset and do what is necessary to smooth ruffled feathers. This may include an apology from the person who made the comment. If you have a repeat offender on your hands or several employees who don't seem to understand the standards, you may need to have sexual harassment training in your department. Talk to your HR department about this.

Substance Abuse

Substance abuse is a reality, and it could end up affecting one of your employees. Your employee handbook probably lists behavior that is grounds for immediate termination, and drug or alcohol use on the job are usually part of this list. However, you have to be careful because substance abusers are considered physically handicapped under the Federal Rehabilitation Act of 1973. You can ask an employee if he or she has been drinking or doing drugs, but you can't accuse him or her of doing so. If you ask and the answer is no, you have to describe the behavior you observed that led you to ask the question. Regardless of the employee's admission or denial, as a supervisor you can send an employee home for safety reasons due to his or her behavior. However, it is wise to never send a person home alone who is under the influence, because if something happens on the way home, you are liable for it.

If you have an employee who is exhibiting behavior indicative of substance abuse, your company may have a responsibility under state law to help him or her find a treatment program. This would fall under the responsibility of your human resources department.

You can fire an employee whose behavior is inappropriate if it continues and he or she does not seek help. It is important to document every incident and every discussion so that you have a record.

Complaints and Grievances

No workplace is complaint free and you will probably have to deal with complaints or grievances by employees about other employees, about your own behavior, or about job requirements or policies. Because you are the supervisor, you are the one in the line of fire who must listen to these complaints, weigh them, and decide how to proceed with them.

It is important that you encourage comments from your team. Calling them "comments" instead of "complaints" encourages both positive and negative feedback and makes the workplace seem friendlier. You can encourage this by mentioning at a meeting that you welcome comments. You may also wish to ask employees individually if they have any comments, particularly if you're talking to an employee who tends to be quieter than others. Creating an environment where you welcome people's opinions and solicit them will engender a positive feeling, and you'll find you don't just get complaints, but you also get positive feedback.

Listen to all complaints with an open mind and a respectful attitude. Often just being able to vent and clear the air will help an employee feel better about a situation. You need to respond to all complaints that you receive. The best way to handle a complaint is to focus on the complaint and not on the complainer. It is easy to let personalities impact your decision, when in order to handle things in a fair way you need to focus instead on the actual complaint itself. The only time you should let the complainant impact how you view a complaint is if you get one from someone who never complains. This is a red flag that there is either a real problem, or that your employee is having some problems.

Essential ways to deal with a complaint:

☑ **Act promptly.** Deal with a complaint quickly. Letting it go can be an indication that you don't take it seriously.

☑ **Document everything.** You don't want to ever have your own actions in the situation be called into questions. Keep a record of all responses and actions you take and any further developments.

☑ **Follow company protocol.** If you are required to notify someone else in the company about a complaint, do so promptly. Follow whatever procedure your company requires for formal complaints.

☑ **Gather the facts.** Get details and find out exactly what the problem is, what happened, and what the employee really wants done or changed. Remember that there are three sides to every dispute—the two parties involved, and the truth. People have different perspectives, so try to see things from all perspectives involved.

☑ **Never downplay a complaint.** Doing so will only make the complainer resentful. No matter what the merits are, you need to treat each complaint with equal weight. Direct the right amount of company time and resources to a complaint based on what it is, but make it clear that all complaints receive equal consideration.

☑ **Evaluate the situation using your own judgment.** If it is up to you to make the call about what happened or how to proceed, do so only after careful consideration. Err on the side of caution. Ignoring a valid complaint can set you and your company up for a lawsuit, while at the same time aggressively pursuing a false complaint can create the same kind of trouble.

☑ **Take action you are authorized to take.** Make sure you fully understand your own powers and the authority given to you, and your limitations in the situation. Handle responses in a swift and business-like manner.

☑ **Touch base with the complainant.** A complaint may be resolved in your mind, but until the person who filed it gets information about how it was resolved, it won't be a closed case. Don't leave your employees wondering if you took them seriously.

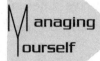

Managing Yourself

When You're in the Hot Seat

If an employee has a comment or complaint about you, take it seriously. You want to create an atmosphere in your team where an employee would feel comfortable coming directly to you with a problem about your own actions or behavior. If there was a misunderstanding, clear it up. If you were at fault, apologize. If a formal complaint is filed about you with the company, document what happened as best you can so that you protect yourself. While such a complaint is being investigated, treat the complaining employee no differently than other employees, but make certain that you are polite and reasonably friendly at all times.

Multicultural Teams

It is a fact that most departments or teams are multicultural, and multicultural teams can provide excellent work environments. If your team currently is not multicultural, it may be wise to ask yourself why that is the case and determine if there are any subtle discriminatory practices in place.

Essentials for leading a multicultural team:

☑ **Set the tone.** As the leader, the attitude you exhibit will be the one your team mimics. Have a positive, supportive attitude toward all team members. If you find working with a multicultural team to be a difficult and unpleasant challenge, your team will never view it any other way. If you view the multicultural team as a unique grouping of people and talents that benefit the company, your team will feel the same way.

☑ **Create a learning environment.** View the different nationalities, races, sexes, and ages of your team as a unique opportunity to understand different cultures. This does not mean you single out an employee and say, "So, José, tell us what it's like to be Puerto Rican." Instead, create a community of acceptance and informal sharing that will benefit and enrich everyone's lives.

☑ **Be aware of differences.** Some team members may come from cultures where it is difficult for them to question a person in authority, or may not understand unspoken procedures or niceties. Be alert for these kinds of cultural differences, and be ready to convey expectations in words so that they are clear.

☑ **Avoid stereotyping.** Everyone has subtle prejudices that they may not even be aware of. As the team leader, it is your role to treat all employees with equal respect and to manage them in a fair way. Try to recognize if you do have any prejudices and strive to overcome them.

☑ **Repair misunderstandings.** Should a misunderstanding occur between employees, which is somehow tied to their cultural differences, you must be prepared to intervene. It may be necessary to involve a special counselor or consultant to help ease these kinds of conflicts.

Another factor in multicultural teams is religious differences. It is useful to understand your employees' religious restrictions and requirements if they impact their work schedule or requirements. For example, it is helpful to plan for an employee who takes time off for a religious holiday each year so that you can organize work flow around it. However, just because someone wears a head covering to work or has a last name that is clearly of a certain culture, you should not assume he or she will have particular religious needs. Allow the employee to come to you to request the time off. Another way to handle this is when you first take your job and meet individually with employees to ask every single one of them if they need particular days for religious observances so that you can plan in advance.

Age Gaps

Teams may be diverse in terms of age. If you are managing people younger than yourself, you may experience a cultural gap. You don't have to tune into pop culture to connect with younger employees, but you do need to find a way to connect with them on a personal level. Younger workers are used to having supervisors who are older than they are, and are often comfortable offering respect. Younger workers offer you an opportunity to learn from their educations and skills. Everyone can benefit from this kind of pairing.

If however, you are managing people who are older than yourself, you may encounter some resistance. Particularly if you advanced from within the company and were promoted instead of older workers, there may be resentment.

Essential ways to earn the respect and confidence of older workers:

☑ **Treat them with respect.** Acknowledge they have experience and make that a resource your team uses. Don't dismiss them as old, not in tune with the world, or stuck in their ways.

☑ **Incorporate new ideas while respecting old ones.** You may have terrific new ideas about how to run things in your department, but innovation can sometimes be met with resistance. Instead of presenting your plan as a clean sweep, incorporate some of the older procedures as well.

☑ **Give them time.** It can take time for older employees to warm up to a younger manager. Go about your business with confidence and assurance, and know that their respect will gradually catch up to you.

☑ **Understand technological differences.** One of the greatest gaps between generations is use and understanding of technology. Don't assume that because an older worker will not use e-mail or because he types with two fingers that he is not useful to the company. Assess all of the employee's strengths and weaknesses. Older workers may benefit from training, assistance, or partnering with other employees to help them become more comfortable with technology.

Privacy

Privacy is something that is important to everyone, and is a concern your employees have about their information in company files. A supervisor has access to a lot of information about employees, and treating that information with respect is important. An employee who feels his or her privacy has been violated will not be a very cooperative worker.

Although employers are not specifically covered by the Health Insurance Portability and Accountability Act (HIPAA), a healthcare privacy law that governs how personal health information must be protected, you do want to provide privacy when it comes to healthcare information for your employees. Most of the things that deal with health information will be functions your HR department will deal with, but this does include information about return to work for disabled or injured employees and keeping an employee's health information separate from his or her personnel file. As a supervisor, you should simply plan to keep any information you have about an employee's health or health insurance to yourself.

A company must strike a balance between employees' privacy concerns and the company's business. Employees should know that they can't expect the same level of privacy that they would have at home while they are work.

As a supervisor you have the right to:

- Inspect an employee's work area.

- Read employee e-mails.

- Listen to employee voice mails.

- Examine employee computer files.

Just because you have the legal right to do these things doesn't mean you should. In fact, if you make it a regular practice to do these things, your employees will feel uncomfortable and you will lose an important sense of trust. It may be necessary to institute a policy of random checks to make sure you keep everyone on the up and up, but a constant intrusion into employees' correspondence and work areas will create a hostile workplace. However, as a supervisor, you must have unfettered access to all company work at all times. Encourage your employees to place shared files or items in one place in their work area so that if you or someone else needs to access them, they will be in an easy place that will not require rifling through their drawers.

You also have access to your employees' personnel files that can contain information such as drug test results, Social Security numbers, payroll amounts, and credit information. However, you have a special role with regard to this type of information and are expected to keep it private and not share it with others—this includes other managers and employees.

Employee Correction

Everyone makes mistakes, and as a supervisor, you should think of employee missteps as an opportunity to improve performance and develop a better employee. Too often, managers think that they need to "discipline" employees. Really, what you need to do is create a positive change instead. Employee mistakes are a signal to you that something is not right—either the employee is not receiving the appropriate direction, does not have needed resources, lacks skills, or needs motivation. You need to interpret the signal and get to the root of the problem, so that you can prevent problems from occurring again. Most of these are faults that you as the team leader can change. Sometimes though, you will end up identifying that the employee is not the right fit, and, you'll want to consider moving or firing that employee.

The simplest form of employee correction is simply sitting down with an employee and offering some feedback or criticism. Think about what outcome you want from the meeting. Your goal is to improve the employee, improve your team, and improve your company; it is not to say "I'm right and you're wrong." What you want to do is effect change. When you are talking to an employee in this situation, be sure you take notes (or make them immediately after the conversation) and keep a record of what happened, even if you are not formally writing the employee up.

It can be hard to know when to formally write someone up and when to offer informal feedback. In general, if the employee didn't do something wrong, but didn't perform as well as he could have, informal feedback is best. You can discuss what happened, pinpoint how to improve things, and end by giving the employee encouragement to step it up next time. However, if an employee is not providing adequate work or violates a policy or rule, then a formal write up is necessary. It is also reasonable to give someone a pass on a first mistake, but further infractions should be taken seriously.

If you are going to be writing the employee up, remember that the documentation you are creating is not just insurance if the employee needs to be fired. It is also helpful for the employee to have a formal written description of what went wrong and what needs to be improved. For example, if you place an employee in charge of managing a vendor relationship and direct him to look for better costs, and the employee only offers a vague response on the progress after several requests, you may need to write him up as unprepared and spell out exactly what would be expected of him next time. This then provides a roadmap for changes the employee can follow.

Learn exactly what your HR department requires in terms of write ups and follow their specifications. Writing an employee up is important for company records, but it also is a way to protect yourself. Take accurate notes and complete all forms so there can be no question about what action you took.

If you have an employee who is in trouble and is in danger of being fired and you think you can turn the situation around, try offering very specific goals and tasks for him or her to complete. Improving the situation takes effort on your part and on the employee's part. To a certain extent, you can micromanage this employee to put him or her on a new track. You should also consider whether the employee would be better suited to a different position or different job responsibilities before letting him or her go. Turning around an existing employee can make sense, because not only does firing someone create costs for your employer, but hiring and training someone new impacts productivity. If you can improve what you've got, you will be ahead.

Unions and You

If your employees are union members, you may have the responsibility of dealing with the union steward. Working with unions does not have to be difficult, if you approach it like any other business dealing.

Read the collective bargaining agreement carefully so that you fully understand it. Don't assume the union steward is out to get you. Instead, approach your relationship in a friendly and business-like way. It is likely you will have differences, but they can be worked through. Develop a relationship with the union steward where you are known for always giving things your full consideration no matter what. The tone you set with the union steward will also set the tone for relationships between you and your employees.

Reviews

Reviews are an important way to provide feedback, but they are also an important legal paper trail for all employees. The purpose of a review is to recap how the employee has progressed in the last quarter, half year, or year. In some companies, reviews are also tied to pay increases. Reviews should allow the employee the chance to first evaluate him- or herself and isolate areas where he or she personally sees the need for improvement. The second part of the review is the chance for you as the supervisor to provide your perspective on what the employee has done well and what he or she needs to improve. If salary is part of the review process in your company, that would be the third component.

Essential steps for a successful review:

☑ **Be prepared.** Organize your thoughts and your main points in advance. Take the time to review the employee's file. If you must provide a written review, write this up in advance. This is a formal legal document so it is important to prepare it correctly and accurately. If it needs to be signed by the employee at the end of the meeting, make sure you get the signature.

☑ **Approach it positively.** Many employees dread reviews. Make it a friendly meeting and go out for a cup of coffee or sit in a conference room so you're not looming from behind a desk. Emphasize the positives when you are able to.

☑ **Be timely.** If an employee is due for a review in March, put it on your calendar and get it done then. Reviews may not seem pressing to you, but they are a sign to your employees that you take their work seriously. Putting them off makes it clear that their job performance is not a priority for you.

☑ **Be specific**. Be prepared to provide examples for your criticisms. Telling someone that they have problems meeting deadlines is vague, but pointing out that they missed deadlines for three specific projects within the last three months helps the employee realize there is a problem. Always provide suggestions for how to improve on the trouble areas.

If reviews are tied to pay increases and your predecessor rubber stamped all increases, you may need to make it clear to your employees that raises will be tied to performance from now on, so that they are not surprised if they do not receive a raise at review time.

Terminating an Employee

Firing an employee is one of the most difficult aspects of being a manager. Nobody wants to be the bearer of bad news, but learning to do this part of your job well is important. If you have laid the groundwork properly, being fired shouldn't be a surprise for the employee at all, because you should have had many conversations about your concerns and offered many chances for improvement.

Before you take the final step of firing someone, make sure you have considered all other options, such as placing that person in a different position or on a different team elsewhere in the company. Because the employee is not a good fit in this particular position does not mean he or she might not excel elsewhere.

Before you fire an employee, you should have detailed records documenting all of the problems you have had with him or her. Talk with your human resources department to learn exactly what the process is and how records must be kept. Documenting everything will solve a lot of the problems involved in firing employees. Not only will they have warning that it is coming, but they will also face a secure paper trail that will make it difficult for them to challenge the firing. Let human resources know when a decision has been made to terminate an employee before you do it.

Usually by the time you've decided you need to fire an employee, he or she is probably aware it is imminent, so it's unlikely it will be a surprise. Because of this, it is a good idea to terminate someone as soon as possible once the decision has been made. Once someone thinks they are going to be fired, they become a negative influence on the team.

Essential ways to make firing easier:

☑ **Do it now.** Putting it off just makes things harder. If you have to do it, get it over with. Some managers find it is easiest to fire someone at the end of the day so that their departure is not as glaring, but in some situations you may need to do it earlier in the day. No matter when you do it, the employee should be told, given the opportunity to gather belongings, and then escorted from the building.

☑ **Plan ahead.** Have documentation ready. Make sure human resources is ready and everyone can do what they need to do once you set the wheels in motion.

☑ **Be succinct.** Say what you need to say and end the conversation. Don't let it turn into a long gripe session by you or the employee.

☑ **Don't discuss it with others beforehand.** Everyone in the office is going to know about it sooner or later, and the reasons for it will probably be clear. Don't talk to your other employees about the firing or the person you have let go.

☑ **Get back to work.** It is normal to feel upset or shaken up when you have to let someone go. It is not a pleasant task no matter what the situation is. You need to force yourself to get back to work and make sure that your employees get back to focusing on work as well. Returning things to normal will help everyone.

After you've terminated a member of your team, you may want to address your team after the fact. While you won't be able to talk directly about the person or the circumstances, you may want to let them know he or she has been terminated in case the news has not traveled. Use this as an opportunity to reinforce what you expect from your team and to focus their attention on goals and positive actions. After an employee has been terminated, don't talk about him or her to other employees if you can avoid it, and don't say anything unkind.

If you must lay off an employee or group of employees, make sure you gather all the information beforehand. Determine who is being laid off, if you can say for how long, and what they will be entitled to in terms of pay and benefits during the lay off period. Be honest, clear, and brief. If this is something you find difficult to do, it is okay to express that, but it should not get in the way of the job you must do and the lay offs you must institute.

I Quit

If you have an employee who makes the decision to leave, you may be shocked, or you may have had some inkling of dissatisfaction. If this is a valuable team member you would very much like to keep, it makes sense to have a conversation about why he or she is leaving and what you might be able to do to keep him or her. Sometimes people become frustrated and quit when talking out the problem and seeing some changes made might resolve the issues for them.

If you can't persuade him or her to stay (or don't want to), consider whether you want the employee to work out the traditional two weeks notice. If you need time to fill the position, want the employee to train the replacement, or you need some time with the employee to go over files or projects, asking him or her to stay is a good idea. Often employees will work the two weeks in exchange for a good recommendation. However, if there is nothing for the employee to do and he or she will just hang around distracting the other employees or spreading dissatisfaction, you should ask the employee to leave as soon as possible.

In the aftermath of an employee quitting, you may have to make some changes to make sure all work is handled until you can fill the position. This may mean asking other team members to take on added responsibilities in the short term.

Chapter 5

Your Plan for Continuing Success

When you take on a new role as a supervisor, you intend to be successful at it, but in the beginning, your focus may be more on learning the ropes, getting to know your team, and laying the groundwork. Once you've reached a point where you're feeling somewhat comfortable in your position, it's time to think about what you can do to ensure that you and your team are successful. It's time to look to the future and make your mark. Becoming a successful supervisor means settling into your new job, but it also means taking your initial success and moving forward with it, so that you display continued results and achievements.

Find Your Successor

You're not even close to thinking about moving on from this job, but you still need to find someone who you can groom to take your job when you eventually leave, whether that is in a year or five years. To do this, you'll want to identify the key people on your team that you can rely on. You don't need to pick one employee, and in fact it is most beneficial to choose several people so that you not only have options, but you also foster some healthy competition. If you clearly pick just one person, you'll end up alienating the others who have potential. Identifying these people is something that will take time to do—you need to observe employees over the long term and notice those who consistently impress you.

Consider your employees. You want to choose ones to mentor who are:

- Smart.

- Efficient.

- Eager to advance.

- Motivated to work.

- Loyal and have integrity.

- Respected by other team members.

- Similar in personality to you.

You don't need to pick people who are necessarily clones of you. It is effective and productive to work with people who have different perspectives, but you may still want to stick with people who share your core approach. Look beyond the obvious—the people you need may not be those who think of themselves as your possible successor. Talent can be found in all corners of your team.

Once you have a few people in mind, try to work directly on projects with them. Daily contact will give you a good feel for how people work and what kind of future they have at the company. You want employees to earn your extra attention over time.

Don't think of it is as choosing someone to succeed you, but instead think of it as finding someone to mentor. If someone has mentored you, you know how helpful it was. Developing these kinds of relationships with employees is beneficial to the team and to the company, because it means you're making long-range plans for stability and success. You're helping your team members improve and grow and are increasing the team's overall assets. It's also helpful for your own success because you develop partners who can work closely with you and implement your vision. And when you are ready to move up in the company, it's easy for your supervisor to find a replacement for you so that you can move upward quickly. And should you move up, you leave behind employees who are loyal and indebted to you.

Essential ways to groom your successor:

☑ **Don't be too obvious.** You don't want everyone to assume you'll always choose Jake for important tasks because he is your obvious favorite. This needs to be a subtle relationship. You also don't want to say to your protégé that you are hoping she will replace you. You can't make promises like that. Keep it low-key.

☑ **Share strategy.** Your successor needs to learn why you make the decisions you do, so talk about the reasons for your choices and present the conflicts you face in making those choices. However, you cannot and should not discuss other employees or any confidential information.

☑ **Offer opportunities.** Give him or her the chance to do new things, learn new skills, and practice new tasks. Provide small opportunities at first and build to greater responsibility. This does not mean shifting your workload to someone else, but allowing him or her to sample a taste of what you do.

☑ **Ask questions.** One of the most important parts of teaching is not simply showing someone how to do something, but questioning them so that they have to think things through on their own. Give your protégé the opportunity to approach problems and find solutions.

☑ **Offer added responsibility.** At times you'll want to give your protégé a taste of management, so allow him or her to experience managing others. You don't want to clearly place this person as your assistant or next in line, but you can allow him or her some responsibility at certain times that involves managing other employees.

☑ **Be accessible.** Make yourself approachable so that this employee can stop by with a question or an idea.

Stay Organized

Everyone comes into a new job with the best of intentions, but it is easy to let your resolution to stay organized fade as you get more involved in your job. While organization is a key component of starting a new job successfully, it is even more important for the long term. The success of a manager will be revealed in his or her organizational skills.

Use the following yes or no questions to help determine if you need an organizational boost:

___Have you or your team missed a deadline in the last six months?

___Do you or team members often have difficulty finding things in your office?

___Are you feeling committed to the organizational system you're using?

___Is your team often unclear about deadlines?

___Do you feel constantly on the edge of losing control of your organizational plan?

___Does your team often ignore the organizational system you have in place?

___Do you find yourself telling your team "Do as I say, not as I do" when it comes to organizational things?

If you answered yes to any of these questions, it is time to reassess.

Essential steps to getting organized:

- ☑ **Make changes.** If you've implemented organizational systems that aren't working, change them. Sometimes we forget that if something isn't working you have to just ditch it and start over, and instead we keep trying to make something work that has no chance of every working out. It takes trial and error to know what will work for you or your team. Before you implement a new organizational system, be sure to evaluate the pros and cons. Get feedback from your team on new systems or plans of organization you are considering. If they've had a voice in choosing it, they will then feel vested in it and more likely to adopt it.

- ☑ **Go electronic.** There are still many managers who do not fully use the capacity of their computers and systems. If you're maintaining lists in notebooks or on pieces of paper, you need to learn to put your computer to work for you. You definitely need to have backups of important documents, files, contact lists, and so on, but maintaining these on the computer means you can't misplace them and will always know where to find them.

☑ **Keep it simple.** Organization has become a big business, and people have a tendency to commit to overzealous, complicated systems. Then, because the systems are too time consuming or confusing, they aren't used and the disorganization continues. An example of a simple organizational plan is the Two Touches Rule. Touch each piece of paper that comes across your desk only twice—once to sort or place it and once to deal with it and send it out. An overly complex organizational system might be one that requires you to record the same information in several places, with the result being that it is too time consuming to do so.

☑ **Make it visual.** Creating a large marker board in the office with deadlines, projects, goals, and other important information visible to all employees is an important way to get everyone on the same page and make this information clear to all. You can also use an organizational tracker on your company intranet, or create a simple board in the office to show how close you are to a goal.

☑ **Create accountability.** It may feel like a hard-nosed approach, but if things are getting lost, billable hours are not getting recorded, or projects are disappearing into no-man's-land, you need to set up a system that will require employees to sign things in and out, to be monitored by software that tracks their time, or that places individuals solely in charge of certain projects. Set up a plan that makes people personally responsible and things will stay much more organized. If you have only one or two people who are having organizational problems, focus on helping them.

☑ **Be open to possibilities.** Not everyone benefits from the same kind of organization, so be aware that what works for some team members may not work for others. Be prepared to use organizational systems that keep the team on track, even though they might not work for you. You can implement personal systems for yourself if you need to, but systems for the whole office should be ones that most employees work well with.

☑ **Stay current.** Keep any organizational system you're using up to date. If you let it slip, it eventually becomes obsolete. You and your team must stay on top of it and enter information, file information, or post information on a regular basis.

Manage Vendors and Suppliers

When people think about being a manager, they often think about managing employees and team members. In actuality, a manager also has to manage relationships with outside people and companies, such as vendors and suppliers, and manage the relationships the team has with these people. These relationships are crucial to your success because they directly impact your profitability, output, and growth.

When working with a vendor, you (or your company) are the customer, so you and your team should be ready for vendors to compete for your business. You're able to choose who you will get your supplies, goods, or services from, and you should be able to negotiate.

Essential tips to keep in mind when choosing a vendor:

☑ **Understand your restrictions.** Your company may have vendors your team is required to work with (common if they are also clients), specific requirements that must be met (such as certain insurance thresholds), or product brands that simply are preferred over others. Know what these restrictions or requirements are and work within them.

☑ **Look at all the factors.** Price is a primary consideration, but so are reliability, delivery time, and quality of work or product. Sometimes you really do get what you pay for. Take all of these factors into consideration when working with vendors or suppliers.

☑ **Monitor employee-vendor relationships.** When you give an employee responsibility to manage contact with a vendor, make sure you keep your finger in the mix. It may be helpful to require your approval for transactions over a certain amount, to sign on with a new vendor, or important orders. Make sure that employees understand how to interact with vendors who are also clients. Also, be sure to occasionally ask employees how vendors are performing, because they may notice changes or problems you are unaware of.

☑ **Have alternatives.** Have backup suppliers for critical components so that your team has other choices in the event the current vendor has a problem. Research these alternatives in advance so you are prepared.

☑ **Get guarantees**. If your team must make commitments to clients based on products from vendors, make sure you, in turn, get a guarantee from the vendors about availability. Before you promise your client 1,000 widgets per week for the next six months, make sure your vendor can guarantee the critical parts.

Manage Clients and Customers

When working with clients and customers, remember they're the ones who pay your salary. However, that doesn't mean your team should be groveling when working with them. Instead, you want to offer a confident, professional, and competent approach that will meet their needs while ensuring your company makes a profit. We like to say that customers may not always be right, but they're never wrong. This is a good rule of thumb when working with a client. You don't ever want to flat out tell them they're wrong; instead you want to steer them toward different considerations.

The whole point of clients is to turn a profit, but you don't want your employees to be completely focused on profit alone when working with customers. They have to strike a balance between service to the customer and profit to the company.

When working with clients, do what you say you will. Don't let your team make promises you know can't be kept. You may win this project, but if you can't deliver, the client will move on afterward. Your company doesn't want to develop a reputation of losing more clients than you can keep. Employees may say what is easiest to keep a client happy without considering the long-term problems. Keep your team focused on what is realistic to promise and what is not.

Place the right employees in contact with clients. There are certain employees who have the right temperament and the right knowledge to work with customers on a regular basis and there are those who do not. Katie may be the best machinist, but she may not be the best person to talk to the client about their piece of equipment.

Designate sales and nonsales employees. Make sure employees are clear about who has authority to discuss price with a customer and who does not. If sales executives are the ones setting all prices, a project manager should never answer a question about price—even a simple one such as "this can't cost more than $10,000 can it?". Give employees the words to use to deflect these inquiries, such as "Every situation is different, so I'll ask the sales executive to get back to you on that question."

Your team must appear confident. If you're always jumping in and offering to beat someone else's price or offer perks a competitor promised, your team isn't going to be bargaining from a very secure position. Decide what you can offer and don't deviate, unless it is in a bargaining situation. Deciding to offer a product or service as a loss leader is a decision that should be made carefully and thoughtfully, and when it is done the reasons for the decision should be communicated to your team. If every price can be negotiated, your clients will think no price is solid.

You must set the tone for how your team members will deal with clients. It is easy for clients to become an annoyance to employees, so it is your role as supervisor to model how to treat them and also to monitor what is happening. You don't want to get a surprise call from your boss chewing you out because one of your team members ignored a concern. If your team is the front line of contact with clients, make sure they understand that they determine the company's image in that client's mind. Many companies now routinely send out surveys to clients to get feedback on customers' experiences, so this is something to consider to help you and your team obtain and react to feedback.

As team manager, you are the head honcho in your department for client contact. As such, it is up to you to maintain a certain level of contact with your clients and customers. Your employees will handle much of the day-to-day work in meeting clients' needs, but as the manager, you need to make it clear to clients that you remain involved, you monitor the work that is done, and that you are always there if there is a concern or question. You don't want to be too hands on though, because you need your team to do the actual work. Your employees should know and understand when it is appropriate to bring you into a situation, and when they should handle it themselves.

Chain of Command

Once you have settled into your position, everyone on your team will obviously know you are in charge. That one's obvious. But part of having a streamlined team is establishing a clear chain of command. There need to be specific people on your team who are the go-to people for certain problems and situations. It makes no sense for an employee to bring an IT problem to your attention when you are simply going to turn around and hand it to your IT specialist. There are certainly situations where you need to be informed of major problems, events, and happenings, but for many tasks, your team members should be able to turn to each other. This may mean specifically designating people to handle particular tasks and making sure everyone knows who is responsible for what. You can portray this as offering a step up in responsibilities and show how it will streamline things for everyone.

Part of having a chain of command is having a reporting sequence in place. Each step of the chain has certain responsibilities and information, but only passes on a small percent of that information to the person above them. Working with your employees to get them to pass the right amount of information up the chain can take some time, but it is worth the effort because it frees you up to handle more important jobs.

To have a solid chain of command, there should be a job description for each employee. Each person should fully understand his or her job description, but should also understand the descriptions for other employees, so that it is clear what responsibilities lie with whom.

Standard Operating Procedures

Standard Operating Procedures, or SOPs, are essential to any well-run team. When you first come into your position as supervisor, there may be some, in place, but as you evolve in your role as manager, you should be able to institute some well-thought-out SOPs. SOPs provide a clear reference for team members as to what is expected of them and how to perform their jobs. They get everyone on the same page so you don't have one person handling things one way while someone else has another method. A smoothly-operating team relies on uniformity to some extent. SOPs should not get out of hand though. You don't want or need them for every little task and function. Use them only when they are useful.

Standard operating procedures are key for job performance ratings. You can compare an employee's performance to what is expected in the SOPs. If things are nebulous, it makes it very difficult to hold an employee up to a standard. SOPs are also very important when you are dealing with issues of safety and mandatory accounting.

Ongoing Learning

In order to grow as people and as employees, we must constantly be learning. Ongoing learning should be an essential part of the plan for success for you and your team. As a manager, you should personally work on developing the skills you have identified as your weaknesses. Take the time now to improve your abilities so that you will be ready for bigger and better jobs down the line. Learn more about your industry. This may mean taking classes, attending seminars, getting another degree, attending training sessions, obtaining certifications, and more. Find out what your company will pay for, and consider what resources you are willing to expend on your own to better your skills. Ongoing learning is an investment in your future.

It is also important for your team to continue to learn and grow. As the team leader, you can teach some skills through meetings and in-house training sessions, but only if they are skills or facts you have a firm grasp on. You can also consider bringing in outside professionals to offer training to your team. Vendors often offer on-site training for new equipment or new techniques and may offer special certifications as well. You may also be able to apply for grants from government agencies to cover the cost of ongoing learning for team members.

Team members can be encouraged to take outside classes and obtain certifications by having the company cover the expense or provide the time off to complete them. Discuss ongoing learning at job performance reviews with your employees. Knowledge and skills that your team members gain are direct benefits to your team and your company.

Benefit the Company, Not the Employees

Ongoing learning has the result of benefiting the company because employees learn new skills or techniques, keeping the company on the cutting edge. The employees also benefit because they gain knowledge and skills that can help them advance. When you're evaluating requests for company-funded continued learning, be on the look-out for requests that are resume-builders, which will be used to help the employee find a new job and not have the effect of improving his or her knowledge and performance in the current job. While employees always benefit from ongoing learning, the essential factor in deciding whether or not to fund such requests should be whether there is a benefit to the company.

Create and Maintain Momentum

Part of achieving success is building momentum. Momentum is a force that keeps you moving ahead. When you are able to generate and support it, it will help you through by overcoming failures and pushing you to greater accomplishments. The hardest part can be getting it started. As with anything, start small. Look for little opportunities to have success. Once you get a few in a row, you can start building towards bigger objectives. Remember that success is truly a journey and not a destination, so momentum must be something you constantly keep in play for you and your team.

Momentum can be generated from personal, team, or company successes. All three are important to the success you are seeking and, to truly make progress, you need all three to coalesce.

Momentum is forward movement. If you are paddling a canoe, it takes a lot of energy to push off and get that canoe moving. Once you've got it going though, it only takes a little energy to keep paddling and continue the forward movement. If you let the canoe stop, you've got exert a lot of energy to get it moving again. As a team leader, you want the team canoe to keep moving forward so that you don't have to restart the momentum. Our motto is *Keep Paddling!*

Once you have started to make some progress (and gain momentum) with your team, work, and projects, don't sit and pat yourself on the back, but use it to keep your forward progress moving. If something worked well, look for opportunities to do more of it. If something didn't work as you would have liked, look for ways to try a new approach. Try to create a habit of success. The momentum it creates will carry you on to more accomplishments and greater rewards.

Remember, not everything will go perfectly. When you encounter bumps in the road or setbacks that could stall your momentum, work to overcome them as quickly as possible. You can navigate around problems if you stay focused on the goals you have set. Bad spells can quickly be turned around if you acknowledge what went wrong and understand why it happened. You can then move on and keep your momentum in full gear.

Set a Pace

While it is important to keep momentum going, it is also important not to burn out. Many new supervisors come into the job all fired up and immediately work themselves into the ground. They also do this with employees—pushing them to the extreme in the beginning, and then watching them peter out. Your success is going to be a long-term proposition; you need to set a pace that you and your team can continue at for the long term. You want to set a pace that allows you to achieve excellence at a level you are comfortable sustaining. You also need to be sure to have a reserve of energy and enthusiasm to help you in any crisis that comes along. As with a runner who has the strength to give it an extra kick as the finish line approaches, keep some energy in reserve so you have the momentum to get to the finish line.

Essential steps for setting a reasonable pace:

☑ **Expend energy equal to the outcome.** Focus the proper level of attention and energy on each project. Understand the importance of your overall goals and don't overemphasize the small tasks.

189

☑ **Allow appropriate playfulness.** You and your employees have to be able to blow off steam at times. Encouraging things such as a relaxed group coffee break, tossing a foam ball around the warehouse, or an afternoon where people slip out early is a good morale booster. When team members have time to enjoy each other's company and take a few minutes without the pressure of work, they rejuvenate themselves. This type of playfulness must be appropriate, not get in the way of other projects, or interfere with the work other team members are doing.

☑ **Have a plan.** Rely on your goals and plan to set your pace. A gradual and consistent movement towards improvement will distinguish you and your team without overtaxing anyone.

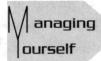

Managing
Yourself

Stress-Busting Tips

➡ **Take deep breaths.** Slowing down and taking the time to breathe will relax your entire body, including your brain.

➡ **Use thought redirection**. When you begin to stress out about something, decide you're just going to stop thinking about it. There is a certain amount of mental processing that is helpful for dealing with problems, but you reach a point where all you do is upset yourself more by thinking about it. Learn to control your thoughts and redirect them to happier topics.

- **Play music.** Relaxing music in the background, or even a couple of songs on an iPod, can crank your stress level down a few notches and help you remain calm.

- **Relax your muscles.** Take a few minutes and work your way through your body, relaxing each area as you go. Reducing physical tension also reduces your mental tension. Stretching is another good way to get some physical relief to tension.

- **Get away.** Take a walk, go on a lunch break, deliver some papers to someone across the building—anything to remove yourself from the physical environment. Even standing up and getting out of your chair can positively impact your frame of mind.

- **Organize your work area.** A messy work area influences your frame of mind. Take a few minutes and straighten things out. It is also helpful to dust once in a while and have the floor swept or vacuumed. When you have a neat and organized area to work in, you will be able to think more clearly.

➥ **Organize your mind.** Take five minutes at the end of the day or at the beginning of the next day to plan out what you need to accomplish in the next day's work. Doing this can allow you to go home at night without a lot on your shoulders because you've already organized it all in your mind before you left. Doing this also allows you to get a glimpse of the big picture and keep things directed towards your main goals.

➥ **Use visualization.** If you are stressing out about a meeting, presentation, or other event, visualize yourself completing it successfully. Studies have shown this will give you extra confidence and help you achieve a successful outcome more easily.

Employee Retention

Hiring good employees and working effectively with your team are two components of success, but to really see success, you need to retain employees. Keeping the majority of your employees does not mean kowtowing to them, but it does mean creating an environment where they are encouraged and supported.

Essential tips for increasing employee retention:

☑ **Make a point of showing appreciation.** Always express your pleasure at how well an employee has performed a task or handled something. We often forget to praise, instead always remember to criticize. Try to flip this and emphasize the positives.

☑ **Create an environment they are proud to be a part of.** Employees must want to see the team succeed and be a part of the success. They need to have ownership in the successes that happen.

☑ **Respond to their needs.** As the team leader, you are in charge of your employees' well-being and satisfaction. If there is something they are not happy about, you are the only one who can turn it around for them, either by making changes yourself, or by reporting the dissatisfaction to higher-ups in the company. Position yourself as the one who solves their problems, and they will want to stay and work for you.

☑ **Anticipate their complaints.** Keep your eyes and ears open and notice problems that are developing or situations that need to be changed before they become huge issues. Heading off problems before they explode will prevent dissatisfaction from beginning. Dissatisfaction is similar to weeds. They are easier to pull when they're small than if you wait for them to spread. The roots will go deep, you'll never dig it all up, and it will keep coming back. You need to keep your ear to the ground and look for clues in order to anticipate these kinds of problems. Having frequent informal conversations with employees helps.

☑ **Create clear path to advancement.** Make sure employees know that hard work gets them some-where, whether it means promotions, raises, bonuses, or increases in responsibilities.

☑ **Find out why.** If employees do leave, try to find out exactly why. There may be problems you are unaware of that could easily be fixed if you could discover them. Having a frank talk with someone about why they quit can be an eye opener.

☑ **Stay out of the ivory tower.** Sometimes a supervisor can become too insulated from his or her employees. One reaction some people have to stress is to distance themselves from the source of the stress. If you per-ceive your employees as a major cause of stress for you, you may try to get away from them. You are a manager and you have different responsibilities, but part of your job is staying tuned in to your employees. If you become unreachable and distant from them, they will stop relating to you. A huge part of job satisfac-tion is the employee-boss relationship. If your employees lose that personal connection to you, they will begin to feel dissatisfied in their jobs, no matter how well other aspects of work are going.

☑ **Protect your team.** Think of your team as an extension of yourself. If you were being asked to do work you knew you had no time for, you would speak up. You need to do the same for your team. You are the only connection your team has to the rest of the company and you must stand up for your team and protect their best interests when you deal with your own supervisor and other managers within the company. Your loyalty certainly is to the company, but your first priority is to keep your team functioning well at a reasonable capacity.

☑ **Take blame and share success.** A good manager claims team failure as his own fault and shares team success with the entire team.

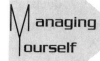

Managing
Yourself

Maintain Balance in Your Life

When you come into a new job, it is normal to focus your priorities and time on it. But as you adjust to the job, you need to continue to have a life and to be a balanced person. You must find time in your life for family, friends, hobbies, activities, vacations, and downtime. Your job is important to you, but it cannot always be everything to you. Taking time to enjoy other things in your life refreshes you and makes you a better supervisor.

Holiday Gifts

The holidays are an emotionally loaded time for many people, and the type of recognition they receive at the office is often a key factor in employee morale. It can be difficult as a new supervisor to know what kind of holiday recognition you should offer to your employees.

Essential guidelines to manage holiday office gifts:

☑ **Find out the status quo.** What did your predecessor do? What happens on other teams and in other divisions? What does your company do for all employees that is not team-specific? You can't make a decision about what you will do until you know the history and the current situation.

☑ **Be consistent.** If you're going to buy gifts or gift certificates for your team members, get everyone the same thing, or things that are clearly of comparable value and thoughtfulness.

☑ **Weigh a gift versus a party.** You may have to choose between getting each employee a gift and having a team employee party. You could take a poll to see what employees prefer. You can also decide what you feel more comfortable offering. It may be possible to compromise and do both on a small scale. Note that many employer-sponsored parties are now being held at other times of the year (to reduce holiday insanity). While this is a good idea, employees are not likely to really consider it a holiday gift or bonus then.

☑ **Distinguish between bonuses and gifts.** A bonus is a company-provided year-end extra, which you as a supervisor have little control of. It may be enough to personally hand out a company bonus to each employee without offering a personal gift as well, but depending on your own financial situation and the size of your team, you may wish to provide something else just from you.

☑ **Be timely.** You don't want you employees to come back to work on December 26th or January 2nd to find a gift from you. It looks like you didn't get your act together or care enough to do it in advance. If you are handing out company bonuses, it is critical that employees get them as soon after they are issued, because many employees count on this money to help with holiday expenses.

☑ **Announce policy changes.** As the economy goes up and down, companies make frequent changes to their employee holiday compensations. If your company usually hands out bonuses, but is cutting back this year, let your employees know this. If your company has always had a big bash, but won't be this year, let people know this so they are not surprised.

☑ **Be sensitive to religious and cultural differences.** Offering a year-end gift may be more appropriate than a Christmas or holiday gift. Make sure that if you designate it as such that you do so for all employees, not just your one Muslim, Hindu, Jewish, or Buddhist employee.

☑ **Don't regift.** Don't ever regift something an employee or boss gave you to another employee or boss.

Deciding whether to buy your own supervisor a gift is a tricky decision. On the one hand, you may want to express your thanks for the new position and the help you've received. But on the other hand, the way business gifts usually work is that the person doing the work receives a gift from the person supervising or hiring them. Gifts normally flow down the corporate ladder, not up. An important consideration is that if you buy your boss a gift this year, you may feel obligated to continue doing it each year, which can get expensive and draining.

Choosing Holiday Gifts for Employees

Good ideas:

✓ Gift certificate to stores, coffee shops, movies, or restaurants.

✓ Mug with candy in it.

✓ Small motivational item for work area (such as a framed saying).

✓ Attractive item useful for your line of work, such as a pen or portfolio.

Bad ideas:

✓ Anything scented or for use in the bathroom.

✓ Clothing (don't try to guess sizes or tastes).

✓ Food (allergies and personal preferences make this impossible).

✓ Items that you received free.

✓ Memberships at clubs or gyms.

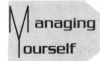

Managing
Yourself

Staying Positive About Your Job

After a while a job becomes, well, just a job. Being promoted or hired is initially very exciting, but the newness wears off and soon you face a daily grind. To continue to be a good supervisor, you must find a way to retain excitement about your job. If you don't feel good walking in the front door of the building most days, your employees won't either, and your team's results will reflect that.

Staying positive about your job doesn't mean you jump up and down and shout "Wahoo!" all the time. It does, however, mean keeping a mindset that allows you to approach work with a level of happiness.

Essential rules to continue a positive mindset at your job:

☑ **Count your successes.** Take the time to tally up what you and your team have accomplished. You've most likely had quite a few successes, and you need to sometimes sit back and contemplate them.

☑ **Have fun.** If you're deadly serious and always under a lot of strain at work, you're not going to want to stay there very long. Relax a little. Have fun with your team and coworkers. Enjoy the parts of your job that are positive. Recognize when it is appropriate to be serious and when some stress relief is called for.

☑ **Decrease pressure on yourself.** When you first come into a job, you feel an enormous pressure to succeed. However, you need to slowly ratchet back that pressure and find a level that is comfortable yet productive.

☑ **Smile.** Research shows that making yourself smile, even when you don't really feel like it, will change your mood and make you happier. Make it a rule that you have to smile a certain number of times per day. Let your employees see you smile so that you can pass the positive energy on.

☑ **Look at the big picture.** There may be things about your job that aren't the greatest, but this job could be your ticket to another promotion, so sticking with it may pay off in the long run. Also, some of the day-to-day things that get you down don't seem that important when you look at things in terms of a five year picture.

Relieve Employee Stress

To help relieve individual employee or team stress:

✓ Tell funny anecdotes that are appropriate for the workplace at the beginning of a tense meeting.

✓ Have a surprise drawing or contest.

✓ Offer unexpected time off.

✓ Buy lunch.

✓ Give personal encouragement.

✓ Make sure employees are not stressing about your reaction to a situation.

Managing Yourself

Develop Confidence

Getting used to a new job takes a few months. Developing confidence can take longer. When you are confident in your role as a supervisor, you will be able to make decisions easier, worry less, and spend less time on certain responsibilities. A confident manager creates a confident team, which in turn produces good work and exceeds goals.

Some people say that confidence is earned, not learned, but we believe that you can train yourself to be confident and have it become a natural reaction. It is possible to be confident even if you know you still have room for improvement. *Everyone* has room for improvement, so that is something that never goes away. However, you can develop confidence in your current skills and achievements.

Confidence is an attitude that will be important to your long-term success. Upper management recognizes confidence in managers and rewards it. Employees also respond better to a boss who is sure and confident. And clients and vendors work better with someone who is clearly confident. There is a fine line between confidence and cockiness.

A confident manger inspires employees to perform better and emulate her style.	A cocky manager alienates employees with his bravado.
A confident manager isn't afraid to acknowledge that he doesn't know something and ask for more information.	A cocky manager hides his ignorance by minimizing the importance of what he doesn't know
A confident manager doesn't need anyone else's praise to feel good.	A cocky manager always looks for the opportunity to one-up an employee or other manager to prove his value.

Essential guidelines to become more confident at work:

☑ **Talk to yourself.** Give yourself mental pep talks. Pat yourself on the back about your achievements. Mentally talk yourself through the steps of the upcoming meeting, presentation, or task that you are preparing for. Use the power of your mind to calm yourself and plant the knowledge that you are successful and are on the path to achieving big goals.

☑ **Use your eyes.** Occasionally stop and look around you. Look at the number of people you have working for you and the trust your company has placed in you. See your office or workspace, parking spot, name plate, or whatever tangible recognition there is of your role as supervisor. Really seeing what you have accomplished will instill confidence.

☑ **Be prepared.** Some people call this the Five Ps: Proper Preparation Promotes Premium Performance. Do your homework. Do everything you need to in advance and you can enter a situation feeling confident and completely ready.

☑ **Face the worst case scenario.** Often people lack confidence because they are too worried about failing. For each project, task, or event you are facing, ask yourself what is the worst thing that could possibly happen. For example, if you're giving a PowerPoint presentation, maybe the worst thing that could happen is the program freezes, or you forget what you were going to say and have to consult your notes. Confront the worst thing that could happen and work through how you would deal with it. Having already solved the biggest problem that could happen, you will have nothing to worry about.

☑ **Fake it.** If you act as though you are confident, people will treat you like you are confident, and soon you will actually become confident. Put on your game face and don't let your worries show, and you will project the right image.

Conclusion

Our intent in writing this book is to provide you with a roadmap to becoming a successful supervisor. We have offered what we believe to be the essential components needed to manage effectively, as you work to attain personal, team, and company goals. While no method is the ONLY way to succeed, there are very specific approaches we believe will help you along the way. Take these ideas and concepts and personalize them to fit your personality and situation.

Supervising can be a rewarding, fulfilling, and enjoyable experience. It can also be difficult, challenging, and exhausting at times. This book has provided you with strategies for success for the good times and the tough times. Whether you will be successful in your role as supervisor is solely determined by you. It is your approach to the tasks before you that will define the type of manager you will become. With proper preparation and execution, there is no limit to what you can accomplish.

A good manager helps the members of the team by supporting, motivating, and guiding their activity and attitudes. A successful supervisor is one who places employees in positions to succeed. By doing this, you will earn the respect of all employees—those who are on your team and those who work with your team.

There will be days where you wonder why you decided to take on this challenge. Remember, you were given this opportunity because others saw the potential in you. You must do the hard work to prove them right. Above all else, you must believe in yourself. There will be mistakes made along the way. Everyone makes mistakes, but it is how you respond that will determine your success. A mistake is an opportunity to learn, and is not a personal failure.

Will every employee agree with you all the time? No, but that's okay. As long as you make your decisions based on careful consideration of the information available, and you do what you honestly believe is the right thing, you will earn their respect. A team that respects you will work hard for you.

As you gain experience as a supervisor, you will learn how best to motivate individual employees. You will find the techniques that help you maximize the productivity of your particular team. You will learn how to keep yourself on track and avoid the distractions that keep you from accomplishing your goals. It takes time and trial and error to learn these things, so you have to be patient with yourself and your team.

As you embark on this next phase of your career, be sure to remember the good things that you did to get here. Many of the skills you used before you became a supervisor will continue to help you in your new role. But also be sure to enhance and augment these with new approaches, techniques, and abilities. As you successfully achieve each goal that you set out for yourself and your team, you will gain confidence and look for more opportunities to grow.

Each day in your career is a building block in your success. We hope this book helps you build your success into a tall and sturdy tower.

Essential Checklists

Essential Things to Note on Your Calendar

☐ Company meetings.

☐ Department meetings.

☐ Employee birthdays.

☐ Supervisor birthday.

☐ Holidays (any that apply to your employees).

☐ Employee vacations/personal days.

☐ Your vacations.

☐ Your supervisor's vacations.

☐ Employee hiring anniversaries for review purposes.

☐ Scheduled retirement dates.

☐ Due dates for reports.

☐ Important project milestones or fulfillment dates.

☐ Vendor contract renewal dates.

Essential Checklist for your Office

- ☐ Paper inbox.
- ☐ Paper outbox.
- ☐ To-be-filed box.
- ☐ Holding box.
- ☐ Up to date employee manuals.
- ☐ Procedure lists.
- ☐ Instructions and warranty for equipment under your responsibilities.
- ☐ Books about your industry/subject matter.
- ☐ Contact information for vendors.
- ☐ Contact information for clients/customers.
- ☐ Contact information for employees.
- ☐ Calendar.
- ☐ Inspirational items.
- ☐ Portfolio to take to meetings.
- ☐ Business journal to record daily activity.
- ☐ Office supplies: paper, pens, stapler, ruler, calculator, pencils, erasers, index cards, envelopes, rubber bands, tape, paper clips, and sticky notes.

Essential Interview Checklist

❑ Application.

❑ References.

❑ List of prepared questions.

❑ Tests.

❑ Salary and benefits information.

❑ Job description and responsibilities.

❑ Arrange meeting with other company members if necessary.

❑ Arrange for a private room for meeting.

Essential Meeting With Your Boss Checklist

❑ List of current projects with up-to-date status information.

❑ Questions or concerns from you or your employees.

❑ Potential client/customer issues and proposed solutions.

❑ Know how much time he/she has available for the meeting.

❑ Supporting materials if needed—have them with you or know where they are if he/she asks for them.

❑ Copies of reports/documents relevant to the discussion.

❑ Samples or prototypes necessary for topics to be covered.

❑ Pen and paper.

❑ Your calendar.

Essential Beginning of the Day Checklist

❑ Check your calendar.

❑ Listen to voice mail.

❑ Update your voicemail message.

❑ Create a to-do list of items that need to get done that day.

❑ Read e-mail.

❑ Check in with your assistant, assign tasks, and exchange information and updates.

❑ Check in with your team and assign tasks if needed.

❑ Touch base with other managers or your boss about company issues affecting your team.

❑ Prepare for any meetings.

❑ Follow up on project milestones if any are scheduled.

❑ Complete beginning of daily accounting procedures.

Essential End of the Day Checklist

❑ Update your calendar.

❑ Review your to-do list and move unfinished items to tomorrow's to-do list.

❑ File any reports or correspondence.

- ❑ Check your e-mail.
- ❑ Check your voice mail.
- ❑ Clean off your desk or organize it.
- ❑ Complete batch reports daily accounting procedures.
- ❑ Log off from computer programs or functions that are password protected or secure.
- ❑ Check your calendar for tomorrow.
- ❑ Get materials together for any meetings or tasks scheduled for the following day.
- ❑ Pack any materials you will need at home or before you get to the office in the morning.
- ❑ Do backups, if you are responsible for them.
- ❑ Do any walk-throughs or end of day security procedures you are responsible for.

Essential Meeting Preparation Checklist

- ❑ Create an agenda.
- ❑ Determine the length of the meeting.
- ❑ Identify and inform people who need to make presentations at the meeting.
- ❑ Decide who should attend.
- ❑ Schedule a room or location for the meeting.
- ❑ Put the meeting on your calendar and intranet, if applicable.

❏ Circulate the agenda.

❏ Arrange for technology needed (overhead, projector, computer, conference call, and so on).

❏ Have copies or printouts made for the meeting.

❏ Arrange for refreshments if necessary.

❏ Gather materials needed to bring to the meeting, such as reports, prototypes, and so on.

❏ Mentally plan what you are going to say or visualize your part of the meeting.

Essential Project Checklist

❏ Determine goal for the project.

❏ Confirm deadline for project.

❏ Develop a plan for the project.

❏ Establish milestones.

❏ Identify resources necessary to complete the project.

❏ Execute the plan by assigning project tasks.

❏ Monitor progress.

❏ Complete project.

❏ Evaluate success.

Additional Resources

Business.gov *www.business.gov*

Business Etiquette
www.sideroad.com / Business_Etiquette / index.html

Business Letters *http: / / owl.english.purdue.edu /
handouts / pw / p_basicbusletter.html*

Career Journal.com *www.careerjournal.com /*

Department of Labor Management Occupational
Outlook Handbook *www.bls.gov / oco / oco1001.htm*

Department of Labor Wage and Hour Division
www.dol.gov / esa / whd /

Employment Standards Administration
www.dol.gov / esa /

Fair Labor Standards Act
www.dol.gov / esa / whd / flsa /

Hiring Employees—IRS Guide *www.irs.gov /
businesses / small / article / 0,,id=98164,00.html*

International Business Etiquette
*www.executiveplanet.com /
index.php?title=Main_Page*

Management About.com
http://management.about.com/

Management Books *http://management.about.com/
od/careerdevelopment/tp/TopMgtBooks.htm*

Management Courses Online
*www.worldwidelearn.com/business-course/
management-training-course.htm*

Management Library *www.managementhelp.org/*

Monster.com New Manager Advice
*http://management.monster.com/featuredreports/
new-managers/tentips/*

National Association of Female Executives
www.nafe.com

National Women's Business Council *www.nwbc.gov*

Occupational Safety and Health Administration
www.osha.gov

Sample Business Letters *www.4hb.com/letters/*

Small Business Administration *www.sba.gov*

State Labor Offices
www.dol.gov/esa/contacts/state_of.htm

Small Business Administration Free Online Business
Classes *www.sba.gov/services/training/
onlinecourses/index.html*

Women's Bureau *www.dol.gov/wb/*

Index

About the Authors

Brette Sember is a former attorney and mediator, who mediated for the Better Business Bureau. She is the author of more than 30 books, including *The Complete Credit Repair Kit* (Sourcebooks, 2005), The Divorce Organizer & Planner (McGraw-Hill, 2004), Your Practical Pregnancy Planner: Everything You Need to Know About the Financial and Legal Aspects of Preparing for Your New Baby (McGraw-Hill, 2005), How to Form a Corporation in New York (Sourcebooks, 2003), and many more. She is a member of The American Society of Journalists and Authors (ASJA). Her Website is *www.BretteSember.com.*

Terrence J. Sember holds a B.A. in marketing and an M.B.A. in business management. He has owned and operated two businesses and has more than 15 years experience in management. In addition to his ownership experience, he has held positions including regional sales manager, business development manager, and business consultant, at internet solutions companies; and commercial sales manager at a mobility (accessible vehicle) company. He specializes in business improvement programs. He has managed and motivated sales, clerical, technical support, web production, and art development teams. Terry's successful management of start-up internet solutions companies resulted in sales department revenue of more than $3 million annually (a 100% increase) and a need to double the number of employees. His personal motivational slogan is "Excellence Now."